Essays on J. L. Austin

Essays on J. L. Austin

by

Sir Isaiah Berlin	L. W. Forguson
D. F. Pears	G. Pitcher
J. R. Searle	P. F. Strawson
G. J. Warnock	

OXFORD

AT THE CLARENDON PRESS

1973

Oxford University Press, Ely House, London W. 1

GLASGOW NEW YORK TORONTO MELBOURNE WELLINGTON
CAPE TOWN IBADAN NAIROBI DAR ES SALAAM LUSAKA ADDIS ABABA
DELHI BOMBAY CALCUTTA MADRAS KARACHI LAHORE DACCA
KUALA LUMPUR SINGAPORE HONG KONG TOKYO

Printed in Great Britain
at the University Press, Oxford
by Vivian Ridler
Printer to the University

Foreword

AFTER Austin's death in 1960, and particularly after the publication in 1961 and 1962 of three volumes of his writings, there began, and continued, to appear in philosophical periodicals a considerable body of criticism and commentary on his work; and of course several pieces of that sort had already appeared in his lifetime. The thought behind the original project for the composition and collection of the papers that follow was that a surprisingly large proportion of these critical writings appeared to be somewhat vitiated by misunderstanding—not merely by ordinary misconstrual of what Austin wrote, but, more importantly, by apparent misunderstanding of him and his intentions, of what he had tried to do in philosophy, and of his reasons for so trying. This suggested the idea that it would be desirable and useful to secure the comments of some of those who had had the advantage of, so to speak, observing at close quarters Austin in action, and of having themselves inhabited, in some cases for many years, the philosophical scene in which he was so conspicuous a figure. To have known by personal acquaintance how Austin talked and thought—how, also, he was talked about—over a period of years is, of course, no guarantee of insight or of correct understanding; but it seemed that it would surely make at least more avoidable certain kinds of incomprehension. Further, Austin's personality and his personal position among philosophers in Oxford were unusual and striking, of historical interest and even of historical importance; and it seemed worth attempting to preserve, from oblivion on the one hand or mythology and legend on the other, some sense of what he and his position were actually like, of the impression he made. Accordingly, three of the papers that follow are primarily—though of course on a limited scale and a rather narrow front—prosopographical in character. All of them, with one exception, are by people who had some acquaintance with Austin himself, in some cases over many years; the exception (Professor Forguson) has supplemented comprehensive study of Austin's writings with examination in Oxford of some of his unpublished notes and papers. His contribution to this book, it will be observed, takes the form of commentary on its predecessor by Professor Searle; in every other case, each paper has been composed quite independently of any of the others.

It will be obvious at a glance that the scope of this collection is not in any way comprehensive; and it may even be thought to be regrettably lop-sided in the predominant concern, in its purely philosophical part, with the philosophy of language. This is partly just accidental. Those who were asked to contribute papers were left free to choose the topics on which they would write; it is largely a matter of chance that those whose papers actually materialized had preponderantly chosen topics in the philosophy of language, while those who had considered other topics dropped out. However, it may also be that this apparent imbalance can in part be both palliated and explained by the actual state of current interest in Austin's work; there is good reason to think that, at any rate for the time being, it is his contribution to the philosophy of language that is most highly valued, and most regularly discussed. Concentration on this, then, needs perhaps less apology than might be thought necessary at first sight.

The contributions here by D. F. Pears and Professor Searle have already appeared in print; all the others are printed here for the first time.

G. J. W.

Contents

I

Austin and the Early Beginnings of Oxford Philosophy

SIR ISAIAH BERLIN

THE philosophical trend which afterwards came to be called 'Oxford Philosophy' originated principally in weekly discussions by a small group of young Oxford philosophers—the oldest was 27—which began some time in 1936–7. They were suggested by J. L. Austin who remained their leading spirit until the war brought them to an end. Austin was elected to a Fellowship at All Souls in the autumn of 1933. He had not then fully decided on a philosophical career. He was convinced, so he used to say, that philosophy, as taught in Oxford, was an excellent training for young men; there was no better way of making them rational —in those days his highest term of praise—if only because it generated in them a critical, indeed a sceptical attitude, the only antidote, in his view, to what he called 'being chuckle-headed'. He was to modify his view later: even philosophy as he taught it proved, in his view, helpless against the traditional pieties and naïve beliefs of some of his most gifted pupils. He complained that so far from undermining their conventional opinions, all his efforts left the majority of them incurably respectable and dully virtuous. He knew that he possessed exceptional capacities as a teacher, but he also had a strong desire to do something more concrete and more practical, a job of work, something for which, at the end of the day, there was more to show. He used to tell me that he regretted that he had spent so much time on the classics instead of learning to be an engineer, or an architect. However, it was now too late for that: he was resigned to remaining a theorist. He had a passion for accurate, factual information, rigorous analysis, testable conclusions, ability to put things together and to take them to pieces again, and detested vagueness, obscurity, abstraction, evasion of issues by escape into metaphor or rhetoric or jargon or metaphysical fantasy. He was from the beginning determined to try to reduce whatever could be so reduced to plain prose. Despite his admiration for practical experts, he was, in fact, himself preoccupied by purely philosophical questions, and, when he first came to All Souls, appeared to think about little else. The two living philosophers whom he most admired were Russell and Prichard, the first for his original genius, independence of mind, and powers of exposition; the second because he seemed to him the most rigorous and minute thinker to be found in Oxford at that time. Austin accepted neither Prichard's premisses nor his conclusions, but he admired the single-mindedness and tautness of his arguments, and the ferocity and the total lack of respect for great names with which Prichard rejected obscurity and lack of consistency in philosophy, ancient and modern. His own doctrine of the performative function of words seems to me to owe a good deal to Prichard's painful self-questionings about, for example, the logical character of promises. 'People say that if I say "I agree" to this or that I create rights that were not there before', Prichard would say; '*Create* rights? What does this mean? Blowed if I know.' Austin did not think this, or Prichard's discussion of the nature of moral obligation, to be either unimportant or ill formulated, and talked about it (to me) a great deal in 1933–5.

Our conversations usually began after breakfast in the smoking room at All Souls. When I had pupils to teach I left him by 11 a.m.; but on other mornings I seem to recollect that we often talked until lunch time. He had at that time no settled philosophical position, no doctrine to impart. He would simply seize on some current topic of the day, some proposition uttered by a writer or a lecturer, and cut it into smaller and smaller pieces with a degree of skill and intellectual concentration which I met in no one else until I listened to G. E. Moore. The most admired philosopher of the thirties in Oxford was, I should say, Henry Price, whose lucid, ingenious, and beautifully elegant lectures fascinated his audiences, and were largely responsible for putting problems of perception in the centre of Oxford philosophical attention at this time. The counter-influence, so far as the young philosophers were concerned, was the mounting revolt against the entire traditional conception of philosophy as a source of knowledge about the universe. It was led by A. J. Ayer, whose paper on Wittgenstein's *Tractatus*, read, I think, in the spring of 1932, was the opening shot in the great positivist campaign. *Language, Truth and Logic* had not yet been published; nor had Ryle's views yet advanced, publicly at any rate, beyond *Systematically Misleading Expressions*. Nevertheless the positivist attack, especially in the form of the early articles by John Wisdom at that time appearing in *Mind*, became a source of illumination and excitement to the younger philosophers and of considerable scandal to their elders. A sweeping anti-metaphysical empiricism was gaining converts rapidly. Price alone, at this time, while in some respects an Oxford realist, showed understanding and sympathy for the new movement, and was regarded by its members as something of an ally in the adversary's camp. The movement grew apace. It had invaded the pages of *Mind*, and had its own house journal in *Analysis*. This was a source of deep distress and indeed despair to the most influential among the older Oxford philosophers—Prichard, Joseph, Joachim. They reacted very differently. Joachim, who was one of the last and most scrupulous and civilized representatives of moderate continental Idealism, and lived in a world inhabited by Aristotle, Spinoza, Kant, Hegel, and Bradley, ignored this wave as an aberration, a temporary recession to a crude barbarism and irrationality—a view expressed in their different fashions and more passionately by Collingwood and Mure, although Collingwood thought Ayer a much worthier and indeed more dangerous opponent than Joseph, Prichard, and their disciples. As for Prichard, he evidently felt contempt for and lack of interest in what appeared to him to be the recurrence of fallacies long exposed, something that belonged to a far cruder order of thought than that of the great sophists who opposed the realist philosophy when he was a young man—Bradley and Bosanquet. But he was so intensely preoccupied by his own continuous effort to 'worry things out', as he called it, and so painfully conscious of his own inability to arrive at adequate formulations of the answers to the questions that tormented him, both epistemological and ethical—the former derived from Cook Wilson, the latter from Kant and the Protestant tradition—that he had no time for dealing with confusions and errors of his juniors, most of whom he suspected of wasting their time, and in none of whom he was much interested. The man who suffered most deeply was probably Joseph. He had a very acute sense of the true tradition which he felt it his duty to defend—a tradition which he received at the hands of his deeply admired master Cook Wilson, whose name and fame, despite all his disciples' efforts, are still confined—so far as they survive at all—to Oxford. Plato, Aristotle, to some degree the rationalists, and again Cook Wilson—these Joseph defended to the end of his days. The deadliest enemies of this kind of realist metaphysics were no longer the Idealists, whose day, he agreed with his pupil Prichard, was done, but the empiricists and sceptics headed by the father of fallacies, Hume, followed by Mill, William James, Russell, and other intellectually and morally subversive writers whose doctrines he conceived it as his duty to refute and root out. All his life he had been engaged on the great task of weeding the garden of philosophy; and I believe that there were times when he thought that the great task to which he had been called, of restoring the ancient truths, was at last being achieved, at least in the English-speaking world. But as the twenties wore on, and the thirties began, he saw with horror that rank weeds were springing up again, and not least in Oxford itself, mainly from seeds wafted across from Cambridge—blatant fallacies propagated by Ramsey, Braithwaite, Ayer, and their allies, aided and abetted by various pragmatists in the United States. All these ancient heresies were abroad once more, and evidently influenced the young, as if their shallowness and speciousness had not been exposed over and over again by the faithful band of Cook Wilson's disciples. His last lecture, held in New College garden, was a tremendous onslaught on Russell and Co. He died, I suspect, in a state of intellectual despair—the truth was drowning in a sea of falsehoods, a disaster which he was never able to explain to himself.

Austin was himself one of these dangerous empiricists, although he was not a militant controversialist at this stage; nor was his empiricism inhibited by fidelity to any particular tradition. He was not doctrinaire. He did not hold with programmes. He did not wish to destroy one establishment in the interests of another. He treated problems piecemeal as they came, not as part of a systematic reinterpretation. That effort, in so far as it was made (and of course he did try to develop a coherent doctrine of philosophical method), took place much later. I do not think that I ever heard him say anything during this period, that is, before the beginning of the war, which sprang from, or was clearly intended to support, any kind of systematic view. I do not know whether his pupils in Magdalen will bear me out, but it seems to me that he addressed himself to the topics which were part of the then normal curriculum in Oxford with no conscious revolutionary intent. But, of course, he had a very clear, acute, and original intellect, and because, when he spoke, there appeared to be nothing between him and the subject of his criticism or exposition—no accumulation of traditional commentary, no spectacles provided by a particular doctrine—he often produced the feeling that the question was being posed clearly for the first time: that what had seemed blurred, or trite, or a play of conventional formulae in the books had suddenly been washed away: the problem stood out in sharp relief, clear, unanswered, and important, and the methods used to analyse it had a surgical sharpness, and were used with fascinating assurance and apparently effortless skill. He always, in those days, at any rate, answered one in one's own terminology when he understood what was said to him; he did not pretend that it was not clear until it had been translated into his own language, some special set of terms of his own. In private he used no rhetorical tricks of any kind, and displayed an extraordinary power of distinguishing what was genuine or interesting in what his collocutor said from what was not—from ideological patter, or nervous confusion, or the like. This was not always so in public: opposition made him combative, and in classes or meetings of societies he plainly wished to emerge victorious. But this did not happen, so far as my own experience goes, in private conversation, at any rate not in the presence of those with whom he felt comfortable and unthreatened. I do not mean to say that he was not by temperament dogmatic: he was. But he argued patiently and courteously, and if he failed to convince one, returned to the topic over and over again, with new and highly imaginative examples and first-hand arguments which were intellectually exhilarating whether they produced conviction or not. He still remained throughout this time sceptical about the value of philosophy, except as an educational instrument; but he could not break himself from it: whenever we met during the thirties he invariably found opportunity of raising some philosophical question, and left one not so much with a set of firm and well-argued positions, as with a series of philosophical question marks strewn along the path, which stopped those who listened to him from resting in the comfortable beds of accepted opinion. I think he was much more authoritarian after the war, and did not, at any rate in public, move his pieces until the entire plan of campaign had been thoroughly thought out, and he felt secure against any possible refutation. One of the criticisms made of him—I think a just one—was that he refused to advance rather than face the smallest possible risk of successful counter-argument. Even so, this did not hold so much in private (I speak only for myself); in the thirties his pride and his sense of his own position were not so evidently in play, nor did he conceive philosophy as a set of doctrines and a method to which it was his mission to convert the ignorant and the mistaken. It was not until a later period that his philosophical activity became a consciously planned campaign for the dissemination of the truth.

When Ayer's *Language, Truth and Logic* was published in 1936, Austin expressed great admiration for it, and then proceeded to criticize it, during our afternoon walks, page by page and sentence by sentence, without wishing to score points (he did not get far beyond the first chapter so far as I can remember). Certainly his later polemical ferocity was less in evidence, at any rate so far as the works of his contemporaries—the articles in *Mind* or in *Analysis* on which we fed—were concerned. In 1936, after he had been at Magdalen for about a year, he came to my rooms in All Souls one evening and asked me what I had been reading. Had I been reading any Soviet philosophy and was any of it worth reading? He had visited the Soviet Union as a tourist and had been impressed by his experience. He was attracted by the austerity and sternness and dedication of the grey, impersonal-looking men and women whom he had there seen, had detected the growth of nationalism (of which he did not disapprove) and of admiration (which he shared) for the great men who had worked against gigantic odds, Marx and Lenin for example. His admiration for the founders of communism was, I think, short-lived. His favourite examples of intellectual virtue in later years were Darwin and Freud, not

because he particularly admired their views, but because he
believed that once a man had assured himself that his hypothesis was worth pursuing at all, he should pursue it to its logical
end, whatever the consequences, and not be deterred by fear of
seeming eccentric or fanatical, or by the control of philistine
common sense. If the logical consequences were in fact untenable, one would be able to withdraw or modify them in the
light of the undeniable evidence; but if one failed to explore a
hypothesis to its full logical conclusions, the truth would forever
be defeated by timid respectability. He said that a fearless
thinker, pursuing a chosen path unswervingly against mutter-
ings and warnings and criticism, was the proper object of
admiration and emulation; fanaticism was preferable to
cowardice, and imagination to dreary good sense. What about
Soviet thought? I replied that I had not read anything by any
contemporary communist philosopher which I could genuinely
recommend to him—nothing since Ralph Fox—the only
English Marxist Austin had read or thought worth reading.
But I had a year or two before read an interesting book on
philosophy called *Mind and the World Order* by C. I. Lewis, a
professor at Harvard of whom I had not previously heard. It
says much for the philosophical insulation and self-centredness
of Oxford (and other English universities at that time) that so
little about American philosophy should have been known to
my colleagues and myself. I had come across this book by pure
chance on a table at Blackwell's bookshop, had opened it and
thought that it looked interesting. I bought it, read it, and
thought that its pragmatist transformation of Kantian categories was original and fruitful. I lent it to Austin who left me
almost immediately. He told me that instead of playing his
violin—he used to go through unaccompanied Bach partitas
evening by evening—he began reading it at once. Three days
later he suggested to me that we should hold a class on this book
which had also impressed him.

I may be mistaken about this, but I think that this was the
first class or seminar on a contemporary thinker ever held in
Oxford. Austin's reputation as a teacher was by this time considerable, and a relatively large number of undergraduates
came once a week to our class in All Souls. I had no notion how
joint classes were held, and assumed that their holders would

begin by a dialogue on points provided by the text, in which they would show each other the almost exaggerated respect which was then common form at philosophical debates among dons. Austin opened by inviting me to expound a thesis. I selected Lewis's doctrine of specific, sensible characteristics—what Lewis called *qualia*, and said what I thought. Austin glared at me sternly and said, 'Would you mind saying that again.' I did so. 'It seems to me', said Austin, speaking slowly, 'that what you have just said is complete nonsense.' I then realized that this was to be no polite shadow-fencing, but war to the death—my death, that is. There is no doubt that Austin's performance at our class had a profound and lasting effect upon some, at any rate, of those who attended it. Some of them later became eminent professional philosophers and have testified to the extraordinary force and fertility of Austin's performance. For a performance it undoubtedly was: as much so as Moore's annual classes held at the joint meetings of the Aristotelian Society and Mind Association. Slow, formidable, and relentless, Austin dealt firmly with criticism and opposition of the intelligent and stupid alike, and, in the course of this, left the genuine philosophers in our class not crushed or frustrated, but stimulated and indeed excited by the simplicity and lucidity of the nominalist thesis which he defended against Lewis. 'If there are three vermilion patches on this piece of paper how many vermilions are there?' 'One', said I. 'I say there are three', said Austin, and we spent the rest of the term on this issue. Austin conducted the class like a formidable professor at the Harvard Law School. He put questions to the class. If, petrified by terror, everyone remained silent, he would extend a long, thin finger, and after oscillating it slowly to and fro for a minute, like the muzzle of a pistol, would suddenly shoot it forward, pointing at some man, chosen at random, and say in a loud, nervous voice: '*You* answer!' The victim would, at times, be too terror-ized to utter. Austin would realize this, answer himself, and return to our normal conditions of discussion. Despite these somewhat terrifying moments, the class remained undiminished in numbers and intensity of interest. We spent the term on nominalism. It was the best class that I have ever attended, and seems to me to mark the true beginning of Austin's career as an independent thinker.

At the end of the summer of 1936 Austin suggested that we hold regular philosophical discussions about topics which interested us and our contemporaries among Oxford philosophers. He wished the group to meet informally, without any thought of publishing our 'results' (if we ever obtained any), or any purpose but that of clearing our minds and pursuing the truth. We agreed to invite Ayer, MacNabb, and Woozley, all of whom were at that time teaching philosophy at Oxford; to these, Stuart Hampshire, who had been elected to All Souls, and Donald MacKinnon, who had become a Fellow of Keble, were added. The meetings began some time in 1936–7 (I think in the spring of 1937). They took place on Thursdays in my rooms in All Souls after dinner, and continued, with a few intervals, until the summer of 1939. In retrospect they seem to me the most fruitful discussions of philosophy at which I was ever present. The topics were not carefully prepared, nor necessarily announced beforehand, although I think we knew from week to week what we were likely to talk about. The principal topics were four in number: perception—theories of sense-data as Price and Broad discussed them; *a priori* truths, that is, propositions which appeared necessarily true or false, and yet did not appear reducible to rules, or definitions and what these entailed; the verification and logical character of counter-factual statements which I think, in those days, we called unfulfilled hypotheticals or contra-factuals; and the nature and criteria of personal identity, and the related topic of our knowledge of other minds. When I spoke of perception as one of our subjects, I should have said that what we talked about was principally phenomenalism and the theory of verification with which it was closely bound up, topics on which Ayer held strong, characteristically clear, and well-known opinions. Austin attacked the entire sense-datum terminology, and asked what the criteria of identity of a sense-datum were: if one's field of vision contained seven yellow and black stripes like a tiger skin, did it contain, or consist of, let us say, seven black data and seven yellow ones, or one continuous striped datum? What was the average size of a datum, and what was its average life-span? When could it be said that a single datum changed colour or faded or vanished, or were there as many data as there were hues or saturations of colours or timbres or pitches of sounds?

How did one count them? Were there *minima sensibilia* and did they vary from observer to observer? All this apart from the by that time familiar question, of how the concept of the observer was itself to be analysed. Ayer defended positivism and wished to know, if phenomenalism were abandoned, what was to be put in its place? Did Austin suppose that there existed impalpable substrata either in the old, crude Lockian sense, or in the sense in which some modern scientists and philosophers, who were no less confused and much less consistent or honest than Locke, maintained or presupposed the existence of equally unverifiable and metaphysical entities? I cannot remember that Austin ever tried to furnish any positive answers to these questions or, to begin with at any rate, tried to formulate any doctrine of his own; he preferred, undoubtedly, to drill holes into solutions provided by others. It was, I think, in the course of one of these sceptical onslaughts, after four or five formulations of the reductionist thesis of pure phenomenalism had been shot down by Austin, that Ayer exclaimed: 'You are like a greyhound who doesn't want to run himself, and bites the other greyhounds, so that they cannot run either.'[1] There was certainly something of this about Austin. I do not remember that he did altogether, before the war, come out of the wood on phenomenalism; but he did begin saying even then that he could not see that there was all that much wrong with ordinary language as used about the external world: the problems raised by, for example, optical illusions—double images, sticks bent in water, tricks of perspective and the like—were due to the ambiguities of language, mistakenly analysed by philosophers, and not to implausible non-empirical beliefs. Berkeley, whom he admired as against Locke and Hume, was, in his view, right about this. A stick that was 'really' bent was of course something quite different from a stick 'bent in water', and once the laws of the refraction of light were discovered, no confusion need occur: being bent was one thing, and looking bent was another; if a stick were plunged in water and did *not* look bent, then indeed there would be occasion for surprise. The sense-datum language was a sub-language, used for specific purposes to describe the works of

---

[1] This may have been stimulated by a remark made by Donald MacNabb to the effect that our discussions reminded him of nothing so much as a pack of hounds in full cry (after, presumably, the truth).

impressionist painters, or called for by physicians who asked their patients to describe their symptoms—an artificial usage carved out of ordinary language—language which was sufficient for most everyday purposes and did not itself tend to mislead. As may be imagined, Ayer, and perhaps others amongst us, stoutly resisted this frontal attack upon the view of Moore and Russell, Broad and Price, and the rejection of the entire apparatus and terminology of the English school of the theory of perception. These discussions led to the emergence of 'Oxford Analysis', not so much as a consequence of Austin's specific theses, as from the appeal to common linguistic usage which was made by us all, without, so far as I recollect, any conscious reference at the time to Wittgenstein's later doctrines, even though the 'Blue Book' was already in circulation in Cambridge, and had, I think, by 1937 or so, arrived in Oxford. Similar methods were used in discussing counter-factual statements—their extension and their relation to the verification principle[2]—as well as the problems of personal identity and its relation to memory. If I remember rightly, the principal example of the latter that we chose was the hero of Kafka's story *Metamorphosis*, a commercial traveller called Gregor Samsa, who wakes one morning to find that he has been transformed into a monstrous cockroach, although he retains clear memories of his life as an ordinary human being. Are we to speak of him as a man with the body of a cockroach, or as a cockroach with the memories and consciousness of a man? 'Neither', Austin declared. 'In such cases we should not know what to say. This is when we say "words fail us" and mean this literally. We should need new words. The old ones just would not fit. They aren't meant to cover this kind of case.' From this we wandered to the asymmetry, or apparent asymmetry, between the analysis of propositions made by the speaker about himself and those made by him about others; this was treated from correspondingly differing standpoints by Austin and Ayer, who gradually

[2] If, for example, I were to say 'If a horse called Sylvia runs in this race it will undoubtedly win.' Supposing no such horse ran or even existed, and I am subsequently asked why I thought that it would win. If I answer that I believed this although—or even because—it was an irrational proposition, that I felt inclined to gamble on its truth because I like gambling, that I had not the slightest desire to know whether there was, or could be, any evidence for the proposition, it seems to follow that the meaning of the counter-factual is detached from 'the means of its verification' in however 'weak' a sense, even if the question of its truth is not.

became the protagonists of two irreconcilable points of view. Austin's particular philosophical position was developed, it seems to me, during those Thursday evenings, in continuous contrast with, and opposition to, the positivism and reductionism of Ayer and his supporters. I do not mean to imply that Austin and Ayer entirely dominated the discussions, and that the rest of us were scarcely more than listeners. We all talked a great deal,[3] although if I asked myself what I myself said or believed, apart from criticizing the verification principle, and pure Carnapian logical positivism, I should find it hard to say. All I can recollect is that there was no crystallization into permanent factions: views changed from week to week, save that Ayer and Austin were seldom, if ever, in agreement about anything.

The discussion of what, for short, I shall call *a priori* statements arose out of a paper read by Russell to the Cambridge Moral Sciences Club, which Austin and I attended (in, I think, 1935 or 1936) on 'The Limits of Empiricism'. The thesis was that while such propositions as 'The same object (or surface, or portion of my visual field, or whatever was substituted for this) cannot be red and green at the same time in the same place' appeared to be incontrovertibly true beyond the possibility of falsification, their contradictories did not seem to be self-contradictory. This was so because their truth did not appear to follow from verbal definitions, but from the meaning of colour words, the use of which was learnt or explained by acts of pointing—was fixed by means of what, in those days, used to be called 'ostensive definitions'. The contradictories of such propositions, therefore, seemed better described as absurd or meaningless or unintelligible, and not as contradictions in terms. This stimulated long discussions about verbal and non-verbal definitions; the relation of Carnap's syntactical properties to semantic ones, the difference between the relations of words to words and the relations of words to things, and so on. The dissimilarity of approach between Austin and Ayer once more showed itself very clearly. Ayer, if he perceived that a given theory entailed consequences which, he was certain, were false

---

[3] And interrupted each other unceremoniously; so much so that Austin, with his passion for order, proposed that we 'acquire a buzzer' to introduce discipline. The suggestion was not taken up.

or absurd, for example, the existence of impalpable entities or some other gross breach of the verification principle, even in its so-called 'weak' form, felt that the whole argument must be proceeding on fallacious lines, and was prepared to reject the premisses, and try to think of new ones from which these undesirable consequences would not follow. Austin looked at whatever was placed before him, and was ready to follow the argument wherever it led. It was later maintained by some of his critics (at least in conversation) that this philosophical spontaneity and apparent freedom from preconceived doctrine were not altogether genuine: that in fact they were elaborate Socratic devices which concealed a fully worked-out positive doctrine which he was not yet ready to reveal. I believe this to be false. In 1936–9 he had a philosophically open mind. Indeed, at that time he was full of suspicion of any cut-and-dried doctrine; if anything he seemed to take active pleasure in advancing propositions which appeared to him true or at any rate plausible, whatever havoc they might wreak with the systematic ideas of writers in, say, *Erkentniss* or *Analysis*. He was certainly not free from a certain degree of malicious pleasure in blowing up carefully constructed philosophical edifices—he did like stopping the other greyhounds—but his main purpose seemed to me, then and afterwards, to be the establishing of particular truths with a view to generalizing from them, or eliciting principles at a later stage. He certainly wished to 'save the appearances', and in this sense was a follower of Aristotle and not of Plato, of Berkeley and not of Hume. He disliked clear-cut dichotomies—between, for instance, universals and particulars (as distinguished in C. I. Lewis's book), or descriptive and emotive language, or empirical and logical truths, or verifiable and unverifiable, corrigible and incorrigible expressions—all such claims to clear and exhaustive contrasts seeming to him incapable of doing the job they were expected to do, namely to classify the normal use of words. It seemed to him then, as it did later, that types and distinctions of meaning were often reflected in ordinary language. Ordinary language was not an infallible guide; it was at best a pointer to distinctions in the subject-matter which language was used to describe, or express, or to which it was related in some other fashion; and these important distinctions tended to be obliterated by the clear-cut dichotomies advanced by the all-or-nothing philosophies, which in their turn led to unacceptable doctrines about what there was, and what men meant. Hence when Russell or others gave examples of propositions asserting irreducible incompatabilities between Lewis's *qualia*—colours, sounds, tastes, and the like, propositions which did not seem either analytic, or empirical; or when, to take another example, it was maintained that singular counter-factual statements could not only be understood, but actually believed, even though it was difficult to see how they could be verified, even in principle—Austin seized on these examples and developed them with great force and brilliance, partly, I suspect, from a desire to discover negative instances which would blow up general propositions that had been brought to bear too easily, like distorting moulds, on the complex and recalcitrant nature of things. He had an immense respect for the natural sciences, but he believed that the only reliable method of learning about types of action, knowledge, belief, experience, consisted in the patient accumulation of data about actual usage. Usage was certainly not regarded by him as sacrosanct, in the sense of reflecting reality in some infallible fashion, or of being a guaranteed nostrum against confusions and fallacies. But it was neglected at our peril: Austin did have a Burkean belief that differences of usage did, as a rule, reflect differences of meaning, and conceptual differences too, and thus offered a valuable and relatively neglected path towards establishing distinctions of meaning, of concepts, of possible states of affairs, and in this way did help to clear away muddles and remove obstacles to the discovery of truth. Above all, philosophy was not a set of mechanisms into which untutored expressions had to be fed, and from which they would emerge classified, clarified, straightened out, and cleansed of their delusive properties. In this sense Austin did not much believe in a specifically philosophical technology—the proliferation of gadgets to deal with difficulties. No doubt his insatiable interest in language and philology as such had something to do with this, and his superb classical scholarship fed his inordinate collector's curiosity, at times at the expense of genuinely philosophical issues. Nevertheless, his implicit rejection of the doctrine of a logically perfect language, which was capable of reflecting the structure of reality, sprang from a philosophical vision not dissimilar to that of Wittgenstein, whose then unpublished but illicitly circulated views—for example the 'Blue' and 'Brown' books—had not, so far as I can remember, reached any member of our group before the war. Certainly his first published contribution to philosophy—the paper on 'A Priori Concepts'[4] in which a good deal of his positive doctrine is embodied—owes, so far as I know, nothing to any acquaintance with Wittgenstein's views, unless perhaps, very indirectly, via John Wisdom's articles which he certainly read.

Occasionally those who met on Thursday evenings talked about moral problems, but this was regarded as an escape, not to be repeated too often, from the sterner demands of the subject. We certainly discussed freedom of the will, in the course of which Austin said to me, *sotto voce*, so as not to provoke Freddie Ayer who was at that time a convinced determinist, 'They all *talk* about determinism and *say* they believe in it. I've never met a determinist in my life, I mean a man who really did believe in it as you and I believe that men are mortal. Have you?' This endeared him to me greatly. So did his answer to a question that I once put to him during a walk. I asked: 'Supposing a child were to express a wish to meet Napoleon as he was at the battle of Austerlitz; and I said "It cannot be done", and the child said "Why not?", and I said "Because it happened in the past, and you cannot be alive now and also a hundred and thirty years ago and remain at the same age", or something of the kind; and the child went on pressing and said "Why not?", and I said "Because it does not make sense, as we use words, to say that you can be in two places at once or 'go back' into the past", and so on; and this highly sophisticated child said "If it is only a question of words, then can't we simply alter our verbal usage? Would that enable me to see Napoleon at the battle of Austerlitz, and also, of course, stay as I am now, in place and time?"—What (I asked Austin) should one say to the child? Simply that it has confused the material and formal modes, so to speak?' Austin replied: 'Do not speak so. Tell the child to try and go back into the past. Tell it there is no law against it. Let it try. Let it try, and see what happens then.' It seems to me now, as it seemed to me before the last war, that Austin understood the nature of philosophy, even if he was over-pedantic and over-cautious, and insisted on making over-sure of his defences before plunging into the arena—understood, better than most, what philosophy was.

These discussions were fruitful for several reasons: because the number of those who took part in them was small—it never rose above seven and was usually smaller than that; because the participants knew each other well, talked very freely, and were in no sense on show; they were totally spontaneous, and knew that if they went down some false path which led to a precipice or a marsh it did not matter, for they could retrace their steps, whenever they pleased, in the weeks to come. Moreover, the intellectual freshness and force, both of Austin and of Ayer, were such that although they were in a state of almost continuous collision—Ayer like an irresistible missile, Austin like an immovable obstacle—the result was not a stalemate, but the most interesting, free, and lively discussions of philosophy that I have ever known.

One of the shortcomings of these meetings is something that seems to me to apply to Oxford philosophy in general, at least in those days. We were excessively self-centred. The only persons whom we wished to convince were our own admired colleagues. There was no pressure upon us to publish. Consequently, when we succeeded in gaining from one of our philosophical peers acceptance or even understanding of some point which we regarded as original and important, whether rightly or, as was more often the case at any rate with me, in a state of happy delusion, this satisfied us completely, too completely. We felt no need to publish our ideas, for the only audience which was worth satisfying was the handful of our contemporaries who lived near us, and whom we met with agreeable regularity. I don't think that, like Moore's disciples at the beginning of the century, of whom Keynes speaks in a memoir on his early ideas, any of us thought that no one before us had discovered the truth about the nature of knowledge or anything else; but like them, we did think that no one outside the magic circle—in our case Oxford, Cambridge, Vienna—had much to teach us. This was vain and foolish and, I have no doubt, irritating to others. But I suspect that those who have never been under the spell of this kind of illusion, even for a short while, have not known true intellectual happiness.

II

Austin: a personal memoir

GEORGE PITCHER

In February 1955, Austin came to Harvard, where I was a graduate student, to give a seminar on 'Excuses' and to deliver the William James Lectures. We awaited his arrival with the highest expectations. Word had reached us that Austin was the most interesting philosopher at Oxford and that he dominated the philosophical scene there. This reputation automatically gave him great stature in our eyes, for we all looked upon Oxford as a leading centre of philosophy, and many of us viewed it as *the* place in the world where exciting new work was being done in our subject. Even the very title of his seminar, although it caused derogatory laughter in some conservative quarters, intrigued and delighted the rest of us. We sensed that the arrival of Austin might mean a release from the round of old arguments, a breakthrough to something altogether new. We saw before us the possibility of adventure.

The tiny room C in Emerson Hall was packed with graduate students and faculty members for the first meeting of Austin's seminar. He came in, dressed in a perfectly ordinary, not very well pressed, blue suit, which will always be, in my mind, an essential part of his physical appearance. The first impression he caused in me was one of disturbing incongruity: he looked like an intelligent tax-lawyer, I thought, or a highly competent, perhaps rather too strict, teacher of Latin in a boys' school, but he did not correspond at all closely to my idea of what a distinguished philosopher should look like. He began to talk at once from notes, producing measured phrases and deadly accurate sentences in a lean but not in the least unpleasant tenor voice. He was assured, unflustered, all efficiency and directness. He resorted to no stage effects of any kind, or anyway no obvious

ones: there was something of the dry legal expert in his style as
well as in his appearance.

He first stated his beliefs about the value of paying close
attention to ordinary language, and his reasons for thinking
that the study of excuse-words, in particular, might be philosophically rewarding. These general remarks about the point,
or importance, of the work that lay ahead struck me as being
full of good sense and yet, somehow, not wildly exciting. It was
as if Austin were delivering them from a sense of duty; as if he
thought it was expected of him to reassure us that we were going
to get our philosophical money's worth. But the temperature
immediately rose when Austin got down to matters that obviously lay closer to his heart—namely, to the actual investigation
of ordinary language in the particular area of excuses. He
started with some general comments about excuse-words, and
then, towards the end of the session, introduced us to the work
that was to occupy us for the rest of the term—the attempt to
discover, or uncover, the exact meanings of the various important excuse-words.

What Austin said at that first seminar meeting, and much of
what he was to say later, is now well known, but to us, then, it
was thrillingly new. I clearly remember the exhilaration I felt,
for example, upon hearing that when we qualify an action verb
with an adverb, such as 'voluntarily' or 'involuntarily', we
convert the normal situation into an abnormal one—so that
when, in the ordinary course of events, I just plain yawn or drop
the newspaper beside my chair after reading it, I do it neither
voluntarily nor involuntarily, I just do it. Again, when he told
us the now famous story about two different ways of shooting
the wrong donkey[1]—a story which, in a flash, made it for ever
impossible to think that 'by accident' and 'by mistake' are even
remotely alike, whereas one had previously been inclined to
suppose that they meant the same thing—the ensuing laughter
registered our delighted excitement at this modest, but still
stunning, revelation.

On the emotional graph of my professional life, Austin's
seminar marks a high peak. Here was a daring new way of
doing philosophy—one that seemed to shed light everywhere.
And despite the deliberately self-effacing title 'Excuses', what

[1] *Philosophical Papers*, 2nd edn., p. 185, footnote 1.

we were investigating was far from trivial, for it was nothing less, at bottom, than the concept of human action itself. Using humble but beautifully contrived examples, Austin got us to see the differences between doing something deliberately, intentionally, and on purpose, doing something recklessly, heedlessly, and thoughtlessly, doing something absent-mindedly, inadvertently, and unwittingly—and so on and on. Although of course led by Austin, we all entered into this enterprise with tremendous gusto: hands were constantly being thrust energetically into the air, as we dreamed up fresh examples to formulate, damage, or support a suggestion about what the word(s) currently under discussion meant. We were like children at a party. And yet the serious purpose was accomplished: we were made to see the extraordinary complexity of human actions, their manifold aspects, and the intricate network of ways in which we assess them and their perpetrators.

Part of the fun of Austin's seminar came from his examples and from his striking images. Here is a sample of some that I find recorded in my seminar notes. (I hope they are accurately stated, but I cannot guarantee it.) To show that there is a difference between doing something attentively and doing it with care, he asked us to consider the case of an elderly, conservative motorist who is driving his car very slowly and attentively—but driving it down the very middle of the street. Such a man is not driving with care. In illustrating the differences between intention and purpose, Austin pointed out that a girl's father asks her suitor 'What are your intentions?', not 'What are your purposes?' We spent a lot of time on the differences between the results, consequences, and effects of actions. One of Austin's examples concerning results was this: if some children pick up a mine, play with it, and are killed, this is a result of enemy action; but if an adult picks up a mine, saws it in half, and so is killed, this is *not* a result of enemy action. On another occasion, he remarked that an appeal to 'force of habit' serves as an excuse only if you can explain that the habit, as built up, is, under normal circumstances, all right. So although someone who lights a cigarette in a non-smoking compartment from force of habit has some kind of excuse, it would be no good to offer as an excuse for a murderer that 'He murders people from force of habit'. (He thought of a habit as something super-added to a person's being, something that can be taken on and put off—whence expressions such as 'riding habit' and 'monk's habit'.) In distinguishing between a state of mind and a frame of mind, Austin said that if something puts you in a certain state of mind (depressed, bewildered, agitated), it puts your machinery out of gear, whereas if you are in a certain frame of mind, your machinery isn't out of gear—it is rather in a certain special gear. (He supported this point by reminding us that to say of someone that he is 'in a state', just like that, is to say that he is distressed, upset, in some way out of order.)

At our last meeting we spent a little time trying to figure out what is involved in attempting to do something. We did not reach any conclusions, but among the provocative examples presented for our consideration was this: if a man hacks away with an axe at a pile of logs under the bedclothes, thinking it to be a man in his bed, isn't this attempted murder, despite the fact that the courts hold that it is not? Finally, he left us with an imagined case that still haunts me: Jones is preparing to go on a protracted journey through the desert. He has two enemies, *A* and *B*. *A* treacherously fills Jones's canteen with deadly poison. *B* comes along and, knowing nothing of *A*'s heinous deed, punches a hole in the canteen. Jones marches off into the desert with his leaky canteen and dies of thirst. Question: who killed Jones, *A* or *B*?[2]

By the third or fourth week of term, Austin had made at least one eager convert: I was ready to follow him to the moon. There were others, too, just as willing. Ideally, perhaps, this effect should have been brought about by means of overwhelming philosophical arguments, but in fact it was not, for Austin produced none. Indeed, I cannot recall anything I ever heard, or read, of Austin's that contained a straightforward, old-fashioned philosophical *argument*. Our conversion was effected through what Austin asserted, of course, but it is certain that we would not have reacted to that as we did but for the quite extraordinary, almost palpable, authority with which he

---

[2] I believe that quite a few of Austin's examples were gleaned from law reports and legal text books. In Oxford, he had conducted joint seminars with H. L. A. Hart, who no doubt first brought such sources to his attention. Hart must also have strongly influenced Austin's views about the meaning of many excuse-terms.

asserted it, an authority that seemed uncannily to still all critical doubts while he spoke, causing even his most casual remarks to be received in our minds with a feeling of 'Yes, yes'.

Austin, in any philosophical discussion, was, quite simply, a master—not only in the sense of being expert, but, perhaps even more strikingly, in the sense of being completely in charge. There are many people one can think of to whom one always listens with respectful attention, because what they have to say is generally worth hearing. But the attitude Austin unfailingly elicited from others, students and colleagues alike, went far beyond that. Whenever another member of the group made a comment, one tended instinctively to look at Austin to see what his reaction might be; at all stages of the debate, one eagerly wanted to know what he thought. So, without raising his voice, without resorting to invective or sarcasm, indeed without displaying any of the usual trappings of command, Austin calmly dominated the debates in which he took part. I have never before, or since, witnessed a comparable display of natural authority.

During that spring at Harvard, Austin conducted a series of his famous 'Saturday mornings' with members of the faculty. Two or three graduate students were also invited, and I was lucky enough to be among them. The topic for the term was sense-data; Roderick Firth undertook to make out a case for the legitimacy and usefulness of that concept, and we were to subject it to critical scrutiny. In these discussions the physical and dialectical centre of gravity located itself, predictably, in the person of Austin. He sat in a wooden armchair with the rest of us deployed in a rough semicircle facing him. And the discussion inevitably assumed the shape of the physical layout: the remarks of the others seemed to be directed not to the group as a whole but to Austin, and he answered each one in turn.

One of the most vivid pictures I have of Austin has him on one of those Saturday mornings surrounded by his Harvard colleagues. He is sitting upright, with some notes, which he does not use, on his lap; his legs are crossed, not at the ankle, but at the knee. He is talking quietly, but with great concentration, gazing over our heads towards the back of the room. His eyes gleam with intelligent effort, and his characteristic smile does not betoken levity. In his left hand he holds a filled, unlighted pipe. His right elbow rests lightly on the armrest, and in his hand he holds by the very end, straight up, a burning wooden match. It is the fourth or fifth one he has lighted since filling his pipe; each has burned down, as this one is now doing, alarmingly close to the fingertips. Our attention is about equally divided between what Austin is so intently saying and the progress of the flame down the matchstick. At the last possible moment, and still without looking at it, Austin quite calmly extinguishes the match by slowly shaking it—he does not blow it out. I have always half suspected that this routine was performed, no doubt in great part unconsciously, for the sake of its dramatic effect, which was considerable; but if this was, indeed, a debater's trick, it was, as far as I know, the only one in Austin's repertoire.

I should like to be able to set down a detailed account, or even a sketch, of what was said at those Saturday meetings: but unfortunately, I took no notes, and my memory is almost a total blank. The two or three others who were there whom I have consulted seem to be in the same boat. So it may be that Austin's reflections are permanently lost. This would be a great pity, for, as Firth has said to me in a letter, 'It seems clear that what he was saying is far from adequately represented by *Sense and Sensibilia*. It was a good deal more refined than *Sense and Sensibilia* and much more general in its philosophical import.' Sadly, that is about all my memory yields up, too: a vague awareness that impressive things were said week after week, but no details to corroborate it.

My personal acquaintance with Austin began very soon after he arrived at Harvard. For some months I had been working on my doctoral dissertation, which of course was going to make a major contribution to philosophy. Wittgenstein's *Investigations* had convinced me that words are tools with many different uses. This struck me as an important idea that had not, however, been worked out in anything like the necessary detail: the aim of my thesis was to do that job. On hearing the opening few sentences of the first William James Lecture, I knew that Austin was about to discuss exactly the same problems I was trying to cope with. The title of his series, 'How to Do Things with Words', was chosen, as he explained, for its pragmatic ring, to honour the man for whom the lectures were named: so obviously Austin would be talking primarily about the uses of language. Everyone will understand why this realization produced mixed feelings in my breast: naturally I was thrilled at the certain prospect of learning a great deal about the subject of my dissertation from a philosopher whom I had by then come to regard with something close to awe, and yet, for this same reason, I couldn't help being disturbed by the thought 'What if he has already done it all?' Typically, it was this latter, gloomy consideration that won out: I was sure that Austin's work would render my mostly non-existent thesis unnecessary. Still, I resolved to ask him if he would be willing to talk with me about it; for after all, if the thing had to be abandoned, it would be best to find out at once.

It must have been after his next William James lecture that I nervously approached Austin; I remember walking back with him to Elliot House, where he had rooms, through the grey, wintry, late afternoon light. I was in a state of high excitement, and was probably talking nonsense; but Austin quickly put me at my ease, not only with his unhurried gait and utterly rational discourse, but also—and this characteristic I could not have anticipated—with his quite overwhelming kindness. Of course he would be happy, he said, to read the parts of my thesis that had already been written, and could we meet to discuss them in two weeks' time? Could we meet? Ah, yes!

Exactly two weeks later, Austin and I met after dinner in his rooms at Elliot House. The sitting-room was austerely furnished, and a model of tidiness. Nothing of Austin's own was visible save for a neat row of books on a shelf, and some papers on the desk. Austin had read my manuscript with care, and he made many helpful criticisms. One that I remember well is the following. I had maintained that a word or sentence is a universal, namely, a certain aspect of the structure of the sounds that are made in uttering it or of the marks that are made in writing it. From this it apparently follows that if a person utters the appropriate sounds, he must necessarily be saying the relevant word or sentence. Austin demonstrated the falsity of this view with a simple example. Suppose I ask you 'If cold water is iced water, what is cold ink?', and you reply 'Iced ink'. You would have uttered the *sounds* 'I stink', but not the *words* 'I stink'; rather, in saying the words 'iced ink', you uttered the sounds 'I stink'.[3]

---

[3] The example, I am told, is a well-known British schoolboy joke.

We didn't have time to discuss all of Austin's comments at that first meeting, and arranged to meet again the following week. When I left, he walked with me a little way, as he had some letters to mail. He told me he wrote every day to his wife, and every few days to each one of his four children. This was the first glimpse I had of another side of Austin's life, one that I was later to observe at closer range—Austin as husband and father.

At our next meeting, we finished the work we could not complete the first time. In the course of our conversation, I let it be known that I thought words were tools, with manifold uses. Austin said, 'Let's see what Witters has to say about that', and he reached for his copy of the *Philosophical Investigations*. He read, among others, section 23, where Wittgenstein lists some of the uses of language—giving orders, speculating about an event, play-acting, making a joke, and so on. Austin remarked that these things are all quite different, and can't just be lumped together like that. He then expressed doubts about the tool-hood of words: 'Are you quite sure that "tool" is the right word? Mightn't they be more like something else—utensils, for example?' He suggested that we try to determine what the various possibilities were; accordingly, he leafed through the *Concise Oxford Dictionary* picking out candidates, while I wrote them down. My list contained about thirty words, including 'appliance', 'apparatus', 'utensil', 'implement', 'contrivance', 'instrument', 'tool', 'machine', 'gadget', 'contraption', 'piece of equipment', 'mechanism', 'device', and 'gimmick'. I seem to remember that 'gewgaw' even had its half-serious day in court. We tried to think of examples of each of these, and to determine what the important differences amongst them were. I think we decided that words were probably more like instruments than anything else on the list. I hugely enjoyed this session. I felt as though I had had a private viewing of Austin at work, and of course I was thrilled to have taken part in the effort. And what a joy it was to discover that philosophy—and I desperately hoped that that was what we had been doing—could actually be fun!

Austin's stay at Harvard was a success of impressive proportions. The extremely high standard of precision in the use of words which he displayed and urged in everything he did—

indeed, which he virtually created—could not fail to exert some measure of permanent influence on the subsequent thought of those who heard him. Among the graduate students, he even made a small number of out-and-out, hard-core converts, like myself, to his special way of doing things. There was universal agreement that what Austin did, he did supremely well; but quite a few people weren't sure what it had to do with philosophy, and some were convinced that it had nothing whatever to do with it. (I remember the perplexed looks on the faces of the non-philosophers who heard Austin address an audience one evening on 'Three Ways of Spilling Ink'.)[4] To the best of my knowledge, everyone at Harvard, whether philosophical friend or foe, liked him, though we did so from a respectful distance.

I had been awarded a Sheldon Travelling Fellowship by Harvard for the coming academic year, 1955–6. Even before Austin's arrival, I had made plans to spend the year at Oxford, and had applied to Magdalen College for admission. Naturally, now that I knew Austin, I was more enthusiastic than ever about the idea of spending the year in Oxford.

After he left Harvard at the end of term, I next saw him in August, when I stopped in Oxford very briefly en route to Berlin, where I was to spend a few weeks before returning to England for the academic year. I rang up Austin, as he had instructed me to do, and was cheered as well as moved to hear the genuine friendliness in his voice. He invited me to lunch with his family the next day; I was to come around to Corpus at noon, and he would drive me out to his house in Old Marston.

I was quite unprepared for the Austin household. I'm not at all sure what I expected to find—perhaps I had half foreseen a prim, middle-aged wife, frighteningly intelligent children wearing enormous spectacles, a cool atmosphere of reserve and decorum. Something like that, I suppose. Anyway, I was totally wrong. Austin's wife, Jean, was far from prim, far from middle-aged. As I gladly discovered, she produced in the house a warming atmosphere of kindness in which anxiety and aloofness quickly vanished. The four Austin children—Hal (*née* Harriet, aged 13), Charles (aged 11), Wig (i.e. Richard, aged 8), and Lucy (aged 4)—were all, indeed, intelligent, but there was

---

4 See *Philosophical Papers*, 2nd edn., pp. 272–87.

nothing frightening about any of them, and none wore enormous spectacles. In fact, each in his own quite different way was a thoroughly engaging *person*: I took to them at once. There was one thing they had noticeably in common, but it was certainly not any feature of the absurd image I had half consciously formed of them in advance; it was, rather, what I might as well call—for that is what it was—their happiness. The Austin house as I saw it was sunny with a quiet, assured joy. To be sure, Austin himself had here, as elsewhere, absolute authority; but this authority was by no means exacted from the others—it did not even seem to me to be exercised. It was just lovingly rendered up to him. From that day to this, the Austins have constituted, for me, one ideal of what a family can be. And I was immediately made to feel that it was a family to which, if I wanted, I might consider myself to belong.

During the year that ensued, in addition to attending his lectures and classes, I saw Austin on an average of something like once every two or three weeks. He very kindly volunteered to act as my informal adviser; although he did not read what I was writing on my thesis, we met periodically to discuss the problems that I was wrestling with. I was often invited to have Sunday dinner—in the middle of the day, not in the evening— at the Austins'. On these occasions, the whole family and I would invariably pile into Austin's old pre-war Rover after dinner for an outing. It soon became an essential part of the routine that the old Rover should break down; it would quietly stop some-where along the highway. Austin would get out and fiddle mysteriously with something in the motor; whatever it was he did, it worked every time. I was told that the car broke down only when I was in it; Austin once remarked, as a man express-ing a firm conviction, 'You see, Pitcher, it just doesn't *like* you!'

Sometime in February or March, it emerged that Austin, years ago, used to play the violin. Since I played the piano, I urged him to dig out his fiddle from its storage place in the attic, or wherever, so that we could play some simple violin sonatas together. Austin hesitated, although not very much, and then agreed to the proposal. I bought some easy Corelli and Telemann sonatas, and in the weeks that followed Austin and I had several extremely pleasant sessions playing them in his living-room. I do not know how much he practised alone, but in any case I thought he played the pieces very well indeed for someone who hadn't touched the instrument in years. He seemed to enjoy these sessions as much as I, but I think he never overcame a certain sense of embarrassment about making music in public, as it were.

Austin saw to it that I was allowed to attend the meetings of the dons' philosophy club. At one of them early in the year, Gabriel Marcel read a paper. Austin was present, and in the discussion period, engaged Marcel in debate. One knew that Marcel's gaudy pronouncements must have been distasteful to Austin, but his interrogation, though searching, was calm and polite. I really think Austin was incapable of discourtesy. Through his insistent probing, the meaning of most of Marcel's darker sayings was revealed, usually as platitudinous. It turned out, for example, that when Marcel told us that human freedom is the ontological counter-weight to death, what he meant was that although we all know we are going to die and that there-fore all our efforts are ultimately in vain, we nevertheless invest some things with value through an act of free will.

I have spoken of Austin's natural authority. This authority gave rise to, and was also part of, the public image of Austin as virtually infallible. It was an image that he seems to have felt a deep need to sustain. Thus although his opinions of course sometimes changed, I never once heard him concede, either explicitly or by implication, that he had made a mistake or been in error. So there was an air of superiority, of knowing it all, about him. But no one, to my knowledge, found this offensive; for it was somehow known that Austin engaged privately in severest self-criticism. Indeed, one had a dim awareness that his self-confidence, however much he may have been entitled to it, was in part a brave front put on against inner uncertainties.

Then, too, there was the more than compensating fact of Austin's extraordinary kindness. He did not, perhaps, lavish it widely, but where he did give it, he gave it unstintedly and— one almost wants to say—*expertly*. I mean that his kindness took the form of acts that he knew would give special pleasure or would serve some specific need. It was, in other words, con-siderately given. Here is one minor example of this that dates from the end of my year in England. I was to leave Oxford around the middle of July to spend a few weeks in Italy before returning

to the United States. I would return briefly to London in early
September before boarding my ship in Southampton. The
problem arose of what to do with my heavy trunk; there could
be no thought of carrying it to the Continent, and yet I had
to get it to Southampton in September for the sailing. Austin
solved this problem with no fuss: I was to leave the thing in the
porters' lodge of Magdalen, where he would fetch it in the old
Rover and ship it off to Southampton in time for my sailing.
And this he did. I have no doubt that the porter on duty was
astounded when the White's Professor of Moral Philosophy
came round to collect a student's trunk; but it was typical of
Austin that he would not have seen any oddity in such an action.

The Austin I knew was a man of generosity and goodwill; so
it is a little difficult for me to understand why many of his colleagues should have feared him. Part of the reason may be that
he had no respect for received opinion, or for accepted ways of
doing things, as such. In all matters, he wished to do away with
what he regarded as bad, and to build again on entirely new
foundations. He certainly sought to do this in philosophy, and I
imagine that his programme, so skilfully and authoritatively
pursued, must have frightened many of his fellow philosophers,
since it could easily be viewed as a serious threat to the value of
their work. Austin was in this sense a revolutionary. He once
told me that he thought students should not be introduced to
the standard philosophical works and problems until quite late
in their careers—only after they had studied the philosophically
relevant areas of ordinary language for some years. This radical
side of Austin's nature was dramatically illustrated, I have been
told, during a college meeting in Corpus Christi devoted to
architectural plans for various of the college buildings. After a
long discussion about how much of the President's Lodgings
should be preserved and how much destroyed, in which there
were complicated and apparently irresolvable differences of
opinion amongst the Fellows of the college, the President finally
turned to Austin and asked him what he thought ought to be
done with that building. 'Mr. President', replied Austin in dead
earnest, 'raze it to the ground.' And he was absolutely right!

After my year in Oxford, I saw Austin again only twice. I had
lunch with the family one day in the summer of 1957 while I
was on holiday in England; and in January of 1959, on his way

back to Oxford from Berkeley, Austin stopped at Princeton to give a talk. The next morning he held a discussion with some of the faculty and graduate students, after which Tom Patton and I drove him to Swarthmore, where he had an engagement to speak. At Swarthmore, Austin talked about sense-data. Among other things, he disputed the claim of some sense-datum theorists that statements about sense-data are equivalent to statements that may be made in ordinary English using some such sentence as 'It seems to me now exactly as if I were seeing the cat on the mat'; he wrote this sentence on the blackboard. He argued that the heart of such assertions is the part that comes after the 'as if'; for example, in one sort of standard case, a person who utters this particular sentence is claiming that he is seeing the cat on the mat, and the function of the first half of the sentence is simply to modify the strength of that claim, to express some sort of reservation about it. To sum up his remarks, he turned to the blackboard and clamped his two hands around the words 'It seems to me now exactly as if', saying 'This is the thinking man's filter'; and then, using his hands again as parentheses, but now around the words 'I were seeing the cat on the mat', he said 'But it's what's up front that counts'. (American readers will remember that 'A thinking man's filter' and 'It's what's up front that counts' were two popular cigarette-advertising slogans of the day.)

Austin was at the top of his form, I thought. Never better. We drove back to Trenton and put him on the train for New York. This last meeting with Austin was, for me, from a personal standpoint, profoundly unsatisfactory. There was no time to re-establish old lines of communication; we were not alone for as much as five minutes. It was as if we were strangers—although we both knew that this was not true. One day in February of the following year, while eating a hurried lunch between classes, I overheard a colleague of mine say to another 'Did you know that Austin is dying of cancer?' I had heard nothing of his illness before that moment. And as a matter of fact, the report was inaccurate in one respect: for he was already dead.

Austin played at least two roles in my life; he was a teacher and a friend. I think I can view him fairly objectively as my teacher. His influence in this capacity was both good and bad. In addition to the many solid truths I learned from him, Austin gave me an awareness of, and respect for, subtle distinctions in the meanings of words. Quite generally, he set for me high standards of precision and accuracy in the use of language (and therefore in thought) that have served as salutary checks on my natural propensity for irresponsible excess. The bad part of his influence was no fault of Austin's: it was just that I fell for too long a time completely under his power. I became his disciple. This meant that I had some tendency to accept things he said not so much because of arguments or supporting grounds, but simply because he had said them. In the area of sense-perception, for example, it was as if I thought: 'Well, if Austin is against sense-datum theories, then there can't be much in them.' But even worse was the fact that I imitated Austin; I went on too long trying to do philosophy in the way I fancied that he did it, when I should have been trying instead to forge a style for myself. This was a measure of my own weakness, to be sure, but also of Austin's formidable strength of personality and intellect.

Naturally, the relationship of teacher and disciple could not help affecting our personal feelings for one another. I looked upon him almost in the way a junior officer might regard his respected and benevolent commanding officer. I can't remember ever addressing him by any name; he called me only 'Pitcher', and personal matters were not broached in our conversations. Austin's affection for me was not of course overtly expressed, and yet I knew that it existed. His feelings were hidden behind a wall of old-fashioned English formality—but it was a wall in which there were chinks. For my part, I think I felt something like love for him. I know, anyway, that I have never stopped missing him.

III

Saturday Mornings

G. J. WARNOCK

DURING the 1950s, just before each University term or sometimes in the first week, I and others used to receive from Austin a small card about 'Sat. mng. mtgs.' (*sic*) for the coming term. Usually, I think, all that it conveyed was where and when we were to meet; the question of what we were to do—if it was not just carrying on with what we had been doing the previous term —would be settled by agreement at the first meeting. The stated time was 10.30 a.m. Austin and a few others were usually present then; but one could turn up at any time, or if otherwise occupied not turn up at all, without attracting comment; and although the meetings broke up in time for people to get away to lunch at about one o'clock, there was no sort of obligation to stay to the end. During any Sat. mng. there were pretty constant comings and goings. Except for the fact that one could attend only at Austin's express invitation, it was, ahead of its time, a sort of unstructured talk-in; no one had to be there or stay there; no one read a paper and no one replied; deviations from the agreed topic were frequent, and if there was a fairly well-marked tendency to 'address the Chair', it was by nature and not by convention that that came about.

Philosophers in Oxford at that time had no premises of their own; we met, as did other philosophical societies, in various colleges. The room I remember best was a shabbily comfortable, leathery, Victorian common-room in the front quad of Balliol, secured for our use by R. M. Hare. Less frequently, a rather similar, but smaller and older room next door in Trinity, arranged by Patrick Nowell-Smith. At least one term, a cold and hideous lecture-room, with little desks, also in Balliol. Occasionally, by arrangement with H. P. Grice, we used a rather splendid modern room in St. John's, with a big central table and highly executive chairs, looking like the board-room of a prosperous and soberly go-ahead commercial company. Officially anyway this was the room that Austin favoured; he claimed to regard arm-chairs and an informal *mise-en-scène* as philosophically debilitating, preferring deployment round a table and a more upright posture; somehow, though, it seems usually to have been in the club-like asymmetry of Balliol that we actually met. The explanation of the cold and hideous lecture-room was that, in that term, a blackboard was necessary; exceptionally, and with a certain sense of dogged duty, we had agreed to get ourselves lectured to, on mathematical logic. Marcus Dick, who had recently returned formidably armed in that line from a year at Harvard, was specially invited to come and tell us what we ought to know. That must have been in the very early 1950s.[1]

One recurrent cause of deviation from our agreed term's topic was that at that time the Philosophical Society met, three times a term, on Friday nights; most people (I am afraid that, for one reason or another, the same would seldom be true today) would have been at those meetings; and it was common for the public discussion on a Friday evening to be continued the next morning in our more private gathering. But the discussion, of course, had not always been interesting enough for that to happen.

There were two main respects, neither perhaps very easy to convey, in which these meetings were quite unlike any others that I have attended. The first was a matter of the position of Austin himself. I cannot think of any comparable instance of personal authority so effortlessly exercised. It was not that the proceedings were formally disciplined; on the contrary, they were exceptionally fluid and free, with no formal order at all. Nor were they solemn; on the contrary, they were continuously enjoyable and amusing—*funny*, in fact. Quite apart from the fact that he enjoyed philosophical argument, Austin liked jokes —sometimes really silly jokes, real farcical fantasy (of which the

---

[1] My wife tells me that, some years later, Charles Taylor, then at All Souls, was similarly commissioned to instruct us in Merleau-Ponty's *Phenomenology of Perception*. Since my mind seems blank on this, I incline to think I must have been away.

most representative instances in his writings are to be found, I think, in his paper 'Pretending'). He did not by any means resemble Wittgenstein, as Malcolm reports him,[2] in not liking other people to laugh at what he himself found laughable; indeed, it is not impossible that Malcolm should have had Austin in mind in his sharp reference, in the same passage, to the 'facetious tone' that is 'characteristic of philosophical discussion among clever people who have no serious purpose'. (It is even possible that Austin did not have a 'serious purpose' *absolutely all the time*.) Even so, these discussions were never just casual, and not even really relaxed. Austin's contemporaries and younger colleagues not only felt great respect for the extraordinary freshness and force of his intellectual gifts; it was also entirely out of the question for them not to treat him personally with respect. It was always just a little as if the headmaster were present; however untrammelled the talk might be and however informal the atmosphere, he was still the headmaster, and there were certain kinds of casualness and unbuttoned disorder that, one knew at once, would not really do. It was plain whose the guiding hand was and where the initiative lay. A recurrent proof of this, by which I never ceased to be both amused and impressed, was the extraordinary way in which the atmosphere would change when, as sometimes happened, Austin himself had to leave our meetings early (when he moved from Magdalen to Corpus Christi as White's Professor, he was sometimes involved in the transaction of that college's business on Saturdays); as the door closed behind him, even though the discussion went on without diversion or interruption, there was an unmistakable sense of people slumping more loosely in their chairs, talking rather more impetuously, laughing—sometimes even giggling—with more abandon. They were now out of range of that formidable magnetic field. I was never quite able to decide what Austin himself felt about this, or even how far he was aware of it. Certainly he preferred a certain formality of manners, or at any rate a strictly limited informality, in relation to people who were not—as most of us were not—his personal friends. I think also that he certainly liked authority, and did not pretend otherwise to himself or to anyone else. But I sometimes thought that he did not always realize how effortlessly his

[2] *Ludwig Wittgenstein: a Memoir*, p. 29.

authority was conceded, how unquestioned it was. It is, I suppose, natural enough that his uniqueness, which seemed obvious to us, was not so evident to him. It never crossed our minds, though perhaps it did his, that there might be any other, or rival, Sat. mngs.

The other thing is that these meetings were uniquely free of that combative, gladiatorial style which is so common in philosophical debate, and can be so very wearying. Of course we disagreed a lot; but it was not, so to speak, an axiom that one *had* to disagree, to look out specially for something, in what anyone said, to disagree with. No one was trying to win, no one was conscious of defending a position, there was to be no dialectical victim at the end of the morning, metaphorically stretched on the carpet in humiliating defeat. There were several reasons for this. The most obvious is that, as I mentioned, no one read a paper and no one replied; so that there was not, as so often there is, right at the outset any deliberate taking up of prepared antagonistic positions, thereafter, for the sake of one's credit, to be bristlingly maintained at all hazards (the 'adversary method' of philosophical inquiry, which is not always bad but is not the only possibility). There is the point as well that those who came to the meetings were in any case not predisposed to disagree; some, perhaps all, had at least a natural share of philosophical argumentativeness, but at least there were no standing hostilities, or obvious obstacles in the way of communicative rationality. Austin had, and no doubt knew that he had, critics among philosophers who, for one reason or another, would have had to be described as really hostile, who intensely disliked the sort of thing that he did and his way of doing it (and perhaps him too); not unreasonably, those people were not invited to be present—nor, probably, had they been invited, would they have come. So not only were there no, so to speak, procedural antagonisms set up by the form of the occasions; there were no real antagonisms either. But above all (I shall come back to this) it was taken for granted that the object actually was to reach agreement if possible—not, of course, because agreement is cosy or comforting, but because some point on which, say, a dozen professional arguers reach general agreement stands at least a decent chance of being actually right. Austin once, when asked to state his 'criterion' of philosophical correctness, replied that, well, if you could get a collection of (he said) 'more or less cantankerous colleagues' all to accept something after argument, that, he thought, would be 'a bit of a criterion'. In any case, to get something right, to say something pertinent and true, was what he wanted to do; and this aim, on these occasions at any rate, was generally accepted. We talked in collaboration, not in competition.[3]

Here I must not give a false impression of general sweetness and light, or even of inhumanly unflawed objectivity. Of course Austin did not make the sheer mistake of really believing that we were all equal collaborators; in my view at least, a large part of the point of our being there was that we certainly were not. But also, I think quite often, in bringing up some topic to be talked about, he had already, though he did not at once disclose, a quite definite view as to what should be said about it; and, though sometimes he did not seem to want to show a hand of his own at all, he often knew which way he wanted the talk of the rest of us to be nudged along, and nudged it accordingly. And certainly he did not himself like to be wrong. The capacity to be absolutely unmoved by the fact that a proposition, shown to be untenable, had just been asserted by *oneself* and not somebody else—to say nothing of being positively pleased by that, as Plato says Socrates was—that capacity was not one of Austin's. Not to mind making public mistakes can be an admirable characteristic, not unknown among philosophers though certainly extremely rare; it can also be symptomatic of the less admirable modesty of those who are conscious of having a lot to be modest about—one may just know that, alas, one's being wrong is not particularly interesting. Austin did not feel like that. It mattered to him—and I think he instinctively felt that it just *mattered*—that he should not get things wrong, and it was not at all easy for him to concede, except at his own prompting, that he had. However, since he did not after all very often make mistakes that the rest of us were sharp enough to notice, it was more important in practice that he did not particularly mind being disagreed with. Indeed, he did not mind at all—he rather expected to say things that we should

[3] It is also important that 'Saturday mornings' were not *public* academic occasions. Collaboration with Austin in giving public classes was—as Berlin, Hart, and Grice would testify—an altogether flintier experience.

not all easily swallow, at any rate to begin with; that was part of the idea.

So what, on all these successive Saturdays, actually went on? Since Austin is generally regarded—of course not altogether wrongly—as having had very definite and idiosyncratic views about what might be called (he would have hated the phrase, unless perhaps it had struck him as comical) philosophical methodology, it ought to be stressed that what went on was very often not idiosyncratic at all. We were not always sternly applying the procedural precepts of 'A Plea for Excuses'. Very often this was because we were construing an actual text, and not usually anything very recondite either. My impression is that we discussed most regularly passages in Aristotle's *Nicomachean Ethics*. After 1953, Wittgenstein's *Philosophical Investigations* came up almost as often. At least once, probably earlier, we spent a term on Frege's *Foundations of Arithmetic*, of which Austin had done a translation in 1950. (I remember, for no particular reason, Austin's puzzlement at Frege's apparent demand that a definition of 'number' ought to tell us that Julius Caesar is *not* a number. Why should definitions provide answers to silly questions?) There was Merleau-Ponty. Then, in 1959, I anyway heard here for the first time the name of Chomsky; we devoted the autumn term of that year to *Syntactic Structures*. In such cases the aim was the quite unidiosyncratic one of trying to get absolutely clear on what was said in, and meant by, the text before us, and of considering whether we were convinced or not by what it said; and Austin had no particular nostrums for the pursuit of that aim. But perhaps there is one thing that should be mentioned here. Austin's favoured unit of discussion in such cases was the *sentence*—not the paragraph or chapter, still less the book as a whole. Roughly, he seemed inclined to make the assumption that, as books are written, or anyway printed, as an ordered sequence of sentences, they should be read by taking the sentences *one at a time*, thoroughly settling the sense (or hash) of each before proceeding to the next one. This naturally worked out rather slowly, and that was all to the good; but perhaps it did not always work out ideally well. The *Tractatus* (which I think we never did discuss) is indeed, at least prima facie, constructed with a view to that sort of step-by-step reading; but most writers, some more than others, often say things, whether wittingly or not, that are only fully intelligible in the light of other things that they have not yet said. This did not greatly matter in the case of Aristotle, with the whole of whose text Austin was perfectly familiar, and the rest of us decently so. But the *Investigations*, I think, did not come up looking at their best in this relentless light; and in some other cases one felt that texts before us were being subjected to a concentrated pressure at every point which, poor things, they were not in the least fitted to withstand. I suspect that with Chomsky, too, we should have got on better if we had started with more notion of where these highly unfamiliar-looking sentences were headed.

I mention, again for no better reason than that I happen to remember it, that one of the things in the *Investigations* that we discussed at some length was the account given there of such sentences as 'I have toothache', the whole question of 'reports', 'descriptions', 'expressions' of pain. Stuart Hampshire (at least if I remember the incident right, and I apologize to him if I do not) had seemed to be taking inarticulate indications of pain, such as groans and grimaces, as a kind of pain-*behaviour*, as something that people in pain *do*. Austin said 'Well, you'd be a tartar in the wards, Hampshire—"Lights out, *and no groaning!*"'

But of course there were plenty of occasions on which the discussion did take a turn peculiarly characteristic of Austin, though perhaps not always quite in the way one would have expected. Groping through my imperfect recollections, I find, I think, three different sorts of somewhat idiosyncratic occasions, of which the third and perhaps the second may be found a bit surprising; but first for the expected one.

As one would expect, there certainly were some occasions on which we, in effect, made lists of English words and phrases, and tried more or less minutely to discriminate their senses and to learn from the distinctions encapsulated in their ordinary uses. Three such cases come readily to my mind, and I mention them in what I believe, though not confidently, to have been their chronological order. One of them took its start from the use, apparently as something of a technical term, of the word 'disposition'; this word, around 1950, was very much in the philosophical air as a word of virtue, having been put there, of course, by Gilbert Ryle in *The Concept of Mind*. Austin, who believed that philosophers' technical terms, or ordinary terms used in technical ways, were *liable*—though of course not necessarily—to blur pre-existing distinctions which sometimes ought—though of course not always—to be preserved or at least noticed, wanted to know what dispositions *really* were; and this led us to compare and contrast the word 'disposition' with, for instance, the words 'trait', 'propensity', 'characteristic', 'habit', 'inclination', 'tendency', and others. I remember that Austin called our attention to the use of 'habit' as a word for certain kinds of, as it were, professional dress, or identifying uniform—monks *wear* habits; and to the botanist's way of speaking of the 'habit' of plants. And I remember that he asked us to try to imagine in detail what, say, a lodger in one's house would probably have been up to (*a*) if one complained of his 'nasty habits', and (*b*) if one complained of his 'nasty ways'. We also considered the sentence (Austin's) 'His *susceptibility* to colds renders him unfit to take part in the International Geophysical Year.' Another somewhat similar tract of discussion arose— presumably, though I do not actually remember—from the philosopher's use of 'use' in talking about meaning, perhaps actually from the comparison of words with tools. This went two ways. On the one hand, we tried to think what sort of thing exactly one would expect to be told, under the general heading 'how to use' this or that (would one be told what to use the thing *for*, or merely told about 'the way' to use it—and what would *that* be? Did 'a way to use' differ from 'a way of using'?) On the other hand, we compared and contrasted such substantives as 'tool', 'instrument', 'implement', 'utensil', 'appliance', 'equipment', 'apparatus', 'gear', 'kit'—even 'device' and 'gimmick'.[4] Here I remember Austin inviting us to classify *scissors*; kitchen scissors, I think we thought, were utensils, and garden shears were probably tools (or implements?), but the sort of scissors used in, for instance, dress-making were something of a problem. (Sewing 'materials' would probably *include* scissors, but that is not quite an answer to the question.) And I remember that he asked why, awaiting an operation, one would be

---

[4] I cannot be sure whether this was before or after the conversation in 1955 mentioned by George Pitcher on p. 24 above.

disconcerted if the surgeon said 'Right, I'll just go and get my tools.' Then once—I am really not sure why or in the hope of what—the logician's use of 'class' led us on to a string of such words as 'group', 'set', 'collection' (what sort of thing does one have to do, to be a *collector*?), 'assemblage', 'range', even 'crowd', and 'heap'.

I must confess (no doubt it is a sign of changed times that I use the defensive word 'confess') that I always found this sort of thing enormously enjoyable, exactly to my taste. I did not believe that it was likely to contribute to the solution of the problems of the post-war world; I did not believe that it would contribute, certainly or necessarily, to the solution of any problems of philosophy. But it was enormously enjoyable;[5] it was not easy; it exercised the wits; and those who think they know that it cannot ever be valuably instructive have simply never tried, or perhaps are no good at it. H. P. Grice once said, when he and I had been looking in this manner at some parts of the vocabulary of perception, 'How *clever* language is!' We found that it made *for* us some remarkably ingenious distinctions and assimilations. That, incidentally, was not on a Saturday morning; regrettably, and perhaps surprisingly, we never, I think, took up problems of perception then at all (except for Merleau-Ponty). I remember Peter Strawson saying that he wished we would, that being just the sort of thing that Austin did best. But probably he did not particularly want to go on about topics on which, throughout this period, he regularly lectured.

The second sort of occasion, though a curiously different sort, which was no doubt highly characteristic of Austin, is best exemplified by our grapplings at one time with Aesthetics. Here, as one would expect, Austin was determined to keep us away from generalities about Art and Beauty and Significant Form; we were to find out what sorts of things people *actually* say, and why, in aesthetic appraisal, when the topic is not so grand as to inhibit good sense, or too obviously complex and controversial to admit of any sort of consensus. We looked at an illustrated handbook of industrial design, containing a wide

---

[5] I could even take—though some felt that it was going too far—the question of the difference between 'highly' and 'very'. Why can one be highly intelligent or highly interesting, but not highly stupid or highly dull?

selection of confident aesthetic pronouncements on humble objects of domestic use such as teapots and jugs. (Can it have been in this connection that he offered, as a possible aesthetic maxim, 'If thine enemy shave one side of thy head, turn to him the other also'?) What was curious about this occasion was that Austin, though of course not uninterested in the particular terms used, seemed to be looking for a *standard form* into which all our specimens could be fitted—a form that would mention some physical and some more aesthetic 'quality', and say how the latter was somehow resultant from the former. (A bell will be rung, for those who were present, by the *schema* 'The *w* of the *x* makes the *y* look *z*'—e.g. 'the shape of the handle makes the pot look stable'.) I was puzzled at the time, by this, as I thought untypical, interest in a uniform formula. But perhaps Austin had a *theory* here, in the background: it ought to be remembered that, though he regarded very general theories with instinctive suspicion, and thought that they were often launched into the world prematurely and recklessly, he very often did have such theories at the back of his mind—and very often kept them there.

Thirdly, and differently again, we spent at least one term in the surprising activity of discussing, in an absolutely ground-floor, first-order way, actual moral problems. No doubt the object here was, typically of Austin, to get us at least temporarily to stand back from the theories, and to remind ourselves not how people are said or supposed to think and talk about these matters, but how they (in this case we ourselves) actually do. But what was curious about this occasion was that, so far as I can remember, practically no philosophical conclusions were ever explicitly drawn, nor did I get any impression that Austin had, even at the back of his mind, any particular philosophical lessons that he hoped we should learn. The only explicit impingement on philosophy that I recall was that Austin seemed to regard with a certain irony R. M. Hare's attachment to 'principles', and seemed not to think much of what were offered as examples of such things. (I recall the words 'a tatty little principle'.)[6] But

---

[6] How would one respond, say as an examiner, to the offer of a bribe? Hare (if memory serves) said that he would say 'I don't take bribes, on principle.' Austin said: 'Would you, Hare? I think I'd say "No, thanks".' I hope that Hare will forgive me if this recollection is inaccurate—or even, perhaps, if it is not.

of course it may be that we were all simply diverted from philosophy by the absorbing interest, of quite another sort, of the
things people said; it was indeed fascinating to see, in colleagues
with some of whom one was only, so to speak, professionally well
acquainted, both what they would come up with as palmary
instances of moral dilemma, and what stands they would take
when it came to considering solutions. In those decorous old
days, propriety set certain recognized though unmentioned
limits to the range of moral problems that were openly can-
vassed, nor could Austin—or perhaps any of us—have endured
excursions into actual autobiography; even so, the things people
said were interesting enough, both when they were unexpected
and, in a different way, when they were not. One question we
discussed at length was this. A personal friend has confessed to
me, in strict confidence, something that would be regarded by
most people as much to his discredit; subsequently, and un-
expectedly, he becomes a candidate for election to a Fellowship
at my college and I, as a member of the electing body, am asked
by my colleagues for my candid judgement of him. What do I
do? We considered variants on this theme—What exactly is it
that he has told me? Would the discredit be moral or intellectual? (What is that distinction?) Do I think that my colleagues
would be *right* in thinking him, if they knew all, disqualified
from election, or that they would be *wrong*? Would he, if elected,
do research or teaching? How good is he at his subject anyway?
And so on. One of us, I remember, averred that he would speak
as follows: 'I happen to know something about this man which
most of you would very probably regard as disqualifying him
from election, but I regret that I am not in a position to tell you
what it is.' We did not think much of that. Austin, I remember,
attached great importance to the fact that one had 'admitted to
one's friendship' the imparter of confidences—a transaction of
which he seemed to have an oddly (or perhaps characteristically?) formal conception; and I believe he did not contemplate,
under any variant, that the man's confidence should thereafter
be betrayed, or even inexplicitly alluded to. When asked what
he would do if his colleagues should subsequently find out the
truth and reproach him for his silence, he replied that he would
'brazen it out'. In another connection—a case about the use of
'tainted money' for virtuous ends—he was surprisingly insistent

that, so excessively ready did he think people were cynically to believe the worst of other people, nothing should *ever* be avoidably done to afford them any pretext for doing so. I am not sure what I learned philosophically during that term, but these discussions too were exceedingly enjoyable.

What was it all for? This was actually a question that I did not much raise at the time, because a good enough answer seemed so very obvious—I expected to learn things that I would not have thought of for myself; and I enjoyed it. But even if no one thought about it very much, there was a formal purpose. Invitation to Sat. mngs. was officially confined to those of Austin's contemporaries and juniors (not all of them) who were full-time tutorial Fellows; and this was not just a handy way of restricting the number of those eligible—the idea, not a bad one, was that full-time tutors were more seriously in danger than others of sinking into the condition of weary, repetitive hacks, their interests strait-jacketed by the syllabus of first-degree examinations and their energies sapped by long hours of teaching, and that they more than others needed to be taken out of themselves, to have a weekly shot in the arm. This was why Austin sought, in varying ways and degrees, always to do something new, or, if not that, to try looking at things in some new sort of way; the one thing he did *not* want was to go over, however well he might have done it, just the same ground as we had all been hacking away at in tutorials that week. He did not want us to get set in our ways; and he did not want us to get bored, or exhausted. My evidence would be that he was extraordinarily successful in this aim. If we did not, like fanatical followers of Savonarola, live each week in the light of the sermon of the previous week-end,[7] there were certainly many tutorials of mine that profited at least a little from that borrowed light.

But one can also say something rather less parochial than that; it was not just a matter of refresher-courses for jaded Oxford tutors. As I have said, Austin did not try to use his Saturday mornings—or at any rate, not often—as experimental material for the systematic application of his own ideas about

---

[7] A comparison of Isaiah Berlin's, which he may well not remember; the conversation in which it occurred did not have a wholly serious purpose.

methods. We never, I think, brought dictionaries with us; we seldom made lists. Nevertheless, some of his ideas did operate—inevitably, I suppose—in a sort of guiding role. I think he wanted us to see, not only for our own immediate good but for the sake of the subject, how desirable it was to get out of 'the bogs and tracks' of familiar, time-hallowed, philosophical campaigning. I think he wanted us to see how satisfactory it could be to have before us small, manageable points that could be completely clearly stated and relevantly discussed. I think he wanted to convince us of the possibility of collaboration, and perhaps above all to get us to believe seriously in the possibility of *agreement*. Our meetings were in some ways more like meetings of civil servants, seeking impersonally and anonymously to reach workable agreement on matters of common concern, than like those confrontations of embattled *virtuosi* with which, alas, one is so much more familiar. (That is *really* what was right, and what so often is wrong.) He wanted to accustom us to not getting along very fast, and to not dismissing impatiently, as if we knew *in advance* what was and was not worth looking into, multiplicity of detail—some of which, indeed, would turn out to be of no great significance.

He wanted us to come to think of philosophy as more like a science than an art, as a matter of finding things out and getting things settled, not of creating a certain individual effect. And certainly not as one of the *performing* arts; once, when I saw him in the audience of a very distinguished philosophical performer, he found the spectacle so manifestly intolerable to him that he had to go away—and was not himself play-acting in doing so. He could not bear histrionics.

I remember that he once came back from America—I think in 1956—a good deal perturbed by what he thought to be the increasing prestige there of Arne Naess. This must have been because he thought he saw the right *purpose*—a more empirical, 'objective' way of doing philosophy, offering the hope of getting things actually settled by patient industry—in danger of being compromised by what he took to be radically wrong *methods*. 'It's infiltrating from the West', he said, shaking his head.

I think he disliked above all the perpetual disorder of philosophy, the perennial disagreement and wrangling, the nearly total failure to achieve any solid and permanent advance; and he thought that work in the subject was depressingly under-organized, unbusinesslike, unsystematic—rather as if it were not taken, even by its practitioners, really seriously. He wanted to tidy it up. It does not seem to me at all mysterious that one should feel like that, though it is another question, of course, why he should have minded *so much*.

No doubt I have not made really clear—perhaps in part because I do not really know—why those Saturday mornings seem to me to have been the best of philosophical occasions. It is probably more relevant than I would easily recognize that at that time I was (as were most of us) fairly new to the business and comparatively young, and so quite in general, I expect, more hopeful and impressionable, readier both to enjoy and to be struck by what went on around me. It is perhaps worth remembering that, in the early 1950s, every single person present there, Austin included, was much younger than I am now; most of us had just started, and in a sense the University itself, after the war, had started again. Things are now two decades further along, *nos et mutamur*.[8] It was partly of course a matter of taste. Not everyone, I imagine, found Austin's jokes—including the really silly ones—as funny as I did; nor was everyone immediately attracted (though absolutely no one was unimpressed) by his formidable personality; some even claim not to have believed in his seriousness of purpose, though that complaint itself need not really be taken seriously. Not everyone is fascinated by the endless subtleties of natural languages, or enjoys making lists of words and then putting them through their paces. These were things that gave me, though, much pleasure and satisfaction. But perhaps I am most nearly clear about what I then valued when I ask myself what, now, I am sometimes conscious of missing. Two things come to mind, and they are probably connected. One is that Austin was absolutely first-hand. He was

[8] On this topic, I remember Austin himself once insisting to me, in the cloisters at Magdalen, that not only is youth—*real* youth—a condition both curious and swiftly transient: it is also, he said, impossible properly to remember, or to characterize retrospectively without falsification. My suggestion of George Moore's *Confessions of a Young Man* he dismissed on the ground that its author was too old (over thirty); his own view was that, in the nearly impossible task of portraying real youth, the most nearly successful contender was Lermontov.

not a purveyor or explainer, however competent or critical or learned, of philosophy; he was a maker of it, an actual origin. One had the feeling—not always, but often—that those meetings, which were so unmistakably his own, were not occasions on which philosophy was talked about, or taught, or learned— they were occasions on which it was *done*, at which that actually *happened*, there and then, in which the life of the subject consists, and which ensures that the critics and explainers have something to explain. I seem to have that feeling less often nowadays; on occasions when one had it, it was well worth being there. The other thing—unless perhaps it is really the same thing—is that he was not predictable. There are good philosophers whose next book or paper or remark, however good, is more or less extrapolable from the last two or three; sometimes even one may find oneself feeling, presumptuously no doubt, that one could almost have written or said it for them, by a bit of induction on the basis of what came before. Austin was not in the least like that. In what he wrote, and perhaps even more in what he said, one was constantly struck by things which it would never have occurred to one to say oneself, and which one could not possibly have foreseen, either, that he was going to say. That also is something in which the life of the subject consists.

IV

Austin and 'Locutionary Meaning'

P. F. STRAWSON

I

AUSTIN distinguishes between the 'meaning' of an utterance and its 'force'. The former he associates with the 'locutionary' act performed in making the utterance, the latter with the 'illocutionary' act performed in making it. What does Austin mean by '(locutionary) meaning'? It is not, I think, clear. Various interpretations seem to receive some support from the text of *How to Do Things with Words*; but the text also supplies grounds for rejecting all these interpretations. I shall first try to establish this; and then suggest a compromise construction, in some respects Austinian, which might be, as it were, imposed on the doctrine. Then I shall suggest some reasons, also derived from the text, which Austin might have for rejecting this imposed construction; and argue that they are not good reasons.

But, first of all, by way of providing a framework for this discussion, I shall set up a simple threefold distinction between what purport to be progressively richer senses of the phrase *'the meaning of what was said'*, as applied to an utterance made on some occasion. There are reasons for thinking that this simple framework is itself too simple; that it would need a certain amount of elaboration, or adjustment or loosening-up if it was to fit all cases.[1] Nevertheless I think it applies well enough over a sufficient range of cases to serve its immediate purpose.

So, then, I begin by distinguishing three progressively richer senses of this phrase, 'the meaning of what was said', as used in application to some utterance made on some occasion.

Suppose a sentence *S* of a language *L* to have been seriously

---

[1] See Strawson, 'Phrase et acte de parole', *Langages*, 17 (mars 1970).

uttered on a certain occasion. Suppose someone, X, to possess just that much information, and no more, regarding the utterance; i.e. he knows what sentence was uttered, but knows nothing of the identity of the speaker or the nature or date of the occasion. Suppose X has ideally complete knowledge of L, i.e. a complete mastery of the semantics and syntax of L. Then is there any sense in which X can be said to know *the meaning of precisely what was said on the occasion in question*? We may answer that it depends. It depends on whether S, viewed in the light of X's mastery of the syntax and semantics of L, is seen to suffer from, or to be free from, syntactic and/or semantic ambiguity. If S is free from any such ambiguity, then, in one sense of the phrase, X does indeed know *the meaning of what was said on that occasion*. But if S suffers from such ambiguity—such ambiguity as, for example, the English sentences, 'He stood on his head' or 'The collapse of the bank took everyone by surprise' suffer from —then X does not yet know, in this sense, the meaning of what was said on the occasion in question. For he does not know which of the alternative readings or interpretations of S is the right one. But suppose this ambiguity is cleared up for him. He is told which of the alternative interpretations is correct, i.e. the one intended. Then he learns, in our present sense of the phrase, the meaning of what was said on that occasion. (Granted that he also has ideal knowledge of another language, L', and that L', though it does not preserve all the ambiguities of sentences of L, is equipped with the means for adequate translation of all such sentences, then X knows neither more nor less than he needs to know in order to *translate S*, as uttered on the occasion in question, into a sentence of L'.) Let us say that if X knows, in this sense, the meaning of what was said on the occasion in question, then he knows the sense-A-meaning (or the *linguistic meaning*) of what was said.

Suppose S is the sentence, 'John will get here in two hours from now'. Evidently, in knowing the sense-A-meaning of what was said, X is far from a complete understanding of what was said. For he does not know who was meant by 'John' or what time and place were meant by 'here' and 'now'. But he may become informed on these points; and if he does, then he knows in a fuller sense than sense A the meaning of what was said. Generally, suppose that, with respect to a sentence S uttered on a particular occasion, one learns not only the sense-*A*-meaning of what was said, but also the import of all the demonstrative or deictic elements, if any, and the reference of all the particular-referring elements, if any, contained in *S*. Then one knows, in a fuller sense than sense *A*, the meaning of what was said. Let us call this fuller sense the sense-*B*-meaning (or the *linguistic-cum-referential meaning*) of what was said. (What one learns, in progressing from knowledge of the sense-*A*-meaning of what was said to knowledge of its sense-*B*-meaning is by no means necessary to the exercise of translation of what was said from *L* to *L'*.)

Even if we know the sense-*B*-meaning of what was said, it by no means follows that we have complete knowledge of *how what was said was meant* or of *all that was meant by what was said*. We may not know, for example, how what was said was intended to be taken or understood. We may know that the words 'Don't go yet' were addressed to such-and-such a person at such-and-such a time; and yet not know whether they were meant as a request, as an entreaty, as a command, as advice, or merely as a piece of conventional politeness. This is the dimension of meaning studied by Austin under the title of 'illocutionary force'. There is another, connected but distinguishable, way in which knowledge of what was meant may go beyond grasp of the sense-*B*-meaning of what was said. It may be that the speaker intends to be taken to be implying, or suggesting, by what he says something which does not strictly follow from its sense-*B*-meaning alone, and that what he meant by what he said is not fully understood unless this intention is recognized. Thus, suppose, in discussing the future occupancy of a certain office, I say 'The President has expressed the view that the ideal age for such an appointment is fifty'. Cannot one easily conceive that I was implying that the President's expression of this view was the result of a prior preference on his part for a certain candidate—whose age, as both my interlocutor and myself know, and know each other to know, happens to be precisely fifty?—and that the meaning of what I said would not be fully grasped by my interlocutor if he failed to recognize that he was intended to recognize this implication?

There is a case, then, for introducing a yet fuller sense of the expression 'the meaning of what was said'. Let us call it the sense-*C*-meaning (or *complete meaning*) of what was said. One knows the sense-*C*-meaning of what was said only if one adds to knowledge of its sense-*B*-meaning a complete grasp of how what was said was to be taken and of all that was intended to be understood by it, together with the knowledge that this grasp is complete.

I have spoken of senses *A*, *B*, and *C* of 'the meaning of what was said' as progressively richer or more comprehensive senses of this phrase. It does not follow that knowledge of what was meant in the more comprehensive sense is, in absolutely every case, more comprehensive knowledge. Thus, sometimes, though exceptionally, the move from *A* to *B* may really be no move at all. This may be the case if, for example, *S* is a sentence which expresses, with complete generality and explicitness, a proposition of pure mathematics or a law of natural science; so that, for example, even the tense of the verb lacks any temporal significance. Again, sometimes, the move from *B* to *C* may add nothing to our knowledge *except the knowledge that there is nothing to be added*, i.e. that no qualification or addition is called for to the way in which, on the strength of our *B*-knowledge (which, of course, includes our *A*-knowledge), we should most naturally take the sentence. For there may be nothing *implied* by what is said except by the use of devices the import of which our *A*-knowledge already covers, and there may be nothing in the way in which what is said is intended to be *taken* or *understood* which is not made explicit by devices which our *A*-knowledge embraces. I have in mind the use of such expressions as 'but', 'perhaps', 'although', 'therefore', 'unfortunately', etc.; and that device of which Austin made us particularly aware, viz. the use of explicitly performative formulae, such as 'I warn (you that . . .)', 'I entreat (you to . . .)', 'I acknowledge (that . . .)', etc. Knowledge of the force of these expressions belongs, evidently, to the level of knowledge of sense-*A*-meaning. Perhaps we can say, too, that the use of the ordinary, closed declarative sentence-form carries, at the level of *A*-knowledge, a presumption of *assertion* which may be simply confirmed at the level of *C*-knowledge without addition or modification. But we are to note that even when there is thus nothing to be added to our *B*-knowledge, the knowledge that this is so is itself something additional to the knowledge of the sense-*B*-meaning of what is said. Thus the move from *B* to *C* is always an addition, even if it is only this minimal addition.

These distinctions, as I have remarked, are rather rough and ready and no doubt call for refinement. Yet, within their limitations, they seem reasonably intelligible and seem also to be of some importance for the general theory of language. All I need to claim for them at the moment is that we understand them well enough for it to be reasonable to raise, in relation to them, the question of what Austin means by '(locutionary) meaning'.

II

Some of the things which Austin says might encourage us to suppose that his distinction between '(locutionary) meaning' and '(illocutionary) force' is related to the distinctions I have just drawn in the following way, which I shall call 'Interpretation I'.

Interpretation I. (i) Knowing the locutionary meaning of what has been said is knowing the meaning of what has been said in sense *B* and hence includes all that is included in knowing the meaning of what has been said in sense *A*. Locutionary meaning is the same as sense-*B*-meaning and hence includes sense-*A*-meaning. (ii) Knowing *both* the locutionary meaning *and* the illocutionary force of an utterance, though not, in general, the same thing as knowing the meaning of what has been said in sense *C*, is something wholly included within the latter. It is not in general the same thing, for knowing the meaning in sense *C* includes knowing *all* that was intended to be taken as understood by the utterance (including all that was intended to be taken as *implied* by it), whereas knowing its illocutionary force may not include as much as this. The distinctive feature of the grasp of illocutionary force is that the utterance be grasped as a case of '*x*-ing' where '*x*' is one of the verbs that qualify for inclusion in Austin's terminal lists. Grasping the utterance thus is certainly included in knowing its meaning in sense *C*, though grasping it thus and knowing its sense-*B*-meaning may not together exhaust knowing its meaning in sense *C*.

Of the two parts of this interpretation of Austin's distinction it is (i) above which mainly concerns us now. It is, I said, tempting to suppose that knowing the locutionary meaning of what has been said is the same thing as knowing in sense *B* the meaning of what has been said and hence includes all that belongs to knowing in sense *A* the meaning of what has been said. For does not Austin himself say that the performance of the locutionary act includes (*a*) the uttering of certain vocables or words, 'belonging to and *as* belonging to a certain voca- bulary, in a certain construction, i.e. conforming to and *as* conforming to a certain grammar' and (*b*) the using of those vocables, or of the 'pheme' which they constitute, 'with a certain more or less definite sense and reference'?[2] The word 'sense' is vague enough, certainly; but it does not seem forced or un- natural to interpret this description of the locutionary act as implying that full knowledge of locutionary meaning includes all that belongs to knowing the sense-*A*-meaning of what is said as well as what is added to this when *A*-knowledge is enlarged to *B*-knowledge.

If we accept this interpretation of Austin's distinction, we shall note a certain consequence. We shall note that just as the move from *B*-knowledge to *C*-knowledge of the meaning of what is said may, in some cases, add nothing to our knowledge except the knowledge that there is nothing to be added, so, and *a fortiori*, the move from knowledge of locutionary meaning to knowledge of illocutionary force may, in some cases, add nothing more than this. In general, on this interpretation, the more freely a speaker uses the devices which Austin refers to in Lecture VI as devices for 'making explicit' the *force* of his utter- ance, the narrower will be the gap between knowledge of the locutionary *meaning* of the utterance and knowledge of its illocu- tionary *force*. If I know that someone, somewhere, at some time seriously utters the sentence 'I apologize', I certainly do not know the meaning in sense *A* of what he says unless I know that —in the absence of any contextual indications to the contrary— he (whoever he is) is apologizing (for something, whatever it is). If I know that someone, somewhere, at some time seriously utters the words 'Oh that it were possible to undo things done, to call back yesterday!', I do not know the meaning in sense *A* of what he says unless I know that—in the absence of any

---

[2] *How to Do Things with Words*, pp. 92–3, 95.

contextual indications to the contrary—he is expressing a wish that this were indeed possible or regret that it is not or both. One could say, indeed, on this interpretation of Austin's distinctions, that his discovery of the explicit performative formula was precisely a discovery of one device of peculiar precision for absorbing more and more illocutionary force into locutionary meaning.

But is it clear that this interpretation of Austin's distinction is correct? There are many remarks in the text which may lead us to doubt it. So now I swing to an opposite extreme of interpretation which I shall call 'Interpretation II'. The swing will perhaps be excessive. But it may help us to settle down, somewhere in between, to the right interpretation, if there is such a thing.

Interpretation II. A preliminary pointer to this opposite extreme is a contrast which Austin draws on p. 73 between meaning and force: 'precision in language makes it clearer what is being said—its *meaning*: *explicitness*, in our sense, makes clearer the *force* of the utterance.' The implication here seems to be quite contrary to the noted consequence of the previous interpretation. It seems to be implied, not that the use of linguistic devices for making illocutionary forces *explicit* results in the absorption of illocutionary force into locutionary meaning, but rather that force can *never* be absorbed into meaning, even when made explicit by the use of linguistic devices. Now the devices which Austin mentions as performing 'the same function' as the explicit performative formula (i.e. the function of making force *explicit*) are numerous and various and include, besides the use of the explicit performative formula itself, the use of the imperative mood (presumably some others as well, perhaps all but the indicative, perhaps *all*?); the use of some adverbs and adverbial phrases (e.g. 'probably'); the use of some connecting particles (e.g. 'therefore', 'although', 'moreover'). So now it looks as if knowing the locutionary meaning of what is said includes knowing only so much of what is meant in sense *A* as is left over when the conventional import of all *these* devices is entirely excluded. Locutionary meaning, so far from including all that what is meant in sense *A* includes, includes only a part of it.

But what part? Let us recall that locutionary meaning, though on this interpretation it includes less than all that is meant in sense

A, includes something which lies outside of what is meant in sense *A*. For it includes what is added to what is meant in sense *A* to yield what is meant in sense *B*. It includes the references of what is said. Locutionary meaning is *sense and reference* together. Now the phrase 'sense and reference' has perhaps the power to swing us into another orbit. And we may be confirmed in the belief that we have been swung into the right orbit by the way in which Austin later associates, and contrasts, the locutionary–illocutionary distinction with the original constative–performative distinction. The thought of the purely constative, as that which is just and simply true or false, is really, he seems to suggest, the result of concentrating on the locutionary aspect of some speech acts, on their meaning (sense and reference), to the neglect of their illocutionary aspects; the thought of the purely performative, as that which has nothing of truth or falsity about it, is the result of concentrating on the illocutionary aspect of some speech acts and neglecting the 'dimension of correspondence with facts'.[3]

Pursuing, then, in the light of these hints and suggestions, the attempt to find a clear notion of locutionary meaning, we may hit on something like the Fregean 'thought'. Only in one respect we shall be carried farther than Frege. For Frege, though he allowed that some interrogative sentences (those that permit of 'Yes-or-no' answers) could express 'thoughts', denied this power to imperative sentences and, for example, to sentences expressing desires and requests, on the ground that the question of truth could not arise for them;[4] whereas Austin certainly thinks of utterances of such sentences as having locutionary meaning, sense and reference. The sentences, 'He is, unfortunately, about to pay the bill', 'He is, fortunately, about to pay the bill', 'Is he about to pay the bill?', 'He is, of course, about to pay the bill' might all, presumably, express one and the same Fregean thought and might all, on this interpretation of Austin, be uttered with the same locutionary meaning; but, on this interpretation of Austin, that very same locutionary meaning might belong also to utterances of the sentences 'Pay the bill now!', 'I rule that he is to pay the bill now', 'I advise you to pay the bill now', 'Will you please pay the bill now?', sentences which

---

[3] See the hints and suggestions on pp. 132, 144–5, 147–8.
[4] See 'The Thought: A Logical Inquiry', trans. Quinton, *Mind* (1956), pp. 21–3.

would presumably not be admitted as expressing a Fregean thought at all.

On these lines, I think, we might find a reasonably clear interpretation of the notion of locutionary meaning. Disregarding explicit performatives, abstracting from the significance of grammatical mood, shearing off the implications of such words as 'but', 'therefore', 'perhaps', etc., we note the minimum remaining content of 'sense and reference'; and observe, not only that the very same content may sometimes be dressed as a verdict and sometimes delivered only as an opinion, but also that the very same content may sometimes figure in a request or an order or a piece of advice as well as in a prediction; and we observe that, however it figures and however it is dressed, we may raise the question whether the facts and it correspond to one another in the way in which they do so correspond, alike when a *predicted* act is performed and when a *commanded* or *counselled* act is performed. This content, then, we look for in every utterance in which we can find it and declare, when found, to be the locutionary meaning of that utterance and its constative aspect, the aspect associated with truth and falsity, with the dimension of correspondence with the facts.

But though we might thus find a relatively clear interpretation of the notion of locutionary meaning, it can hardly be said to be clearly the correct one. For while Austin is indeed anxious to find a constative aspect—an aspect of exposure to assessment in the light of the facts—in, say, a piece of advice as well as in a statement, he does not appeal to the fact that advice given may or may not be followed, that it may or may not in *this* way be 'confirmed' by the facts. He appeals instead to the fact that it may or may not be *good* advice, that it may or may not in *this* way be 'supported' by the facts.[5] So in so far as we base our extended-Fregean interpretation of 'locutionary meaning' on the links: locutionary meaning—sense and reference—constative aspect—assessability in the light of the facts, the interpretation collapses. It collapses because it now looks as if we do have to take account of whether the same content is commanded or predicted, say, in order to know *what* we have to assess in this dimension, i.e. in order to know what locutionary meaning is in question.

[5] *How to Do Things with Words*, p. 141.

Interpretation III (?). Can we find another interpretation, intermediate between the two extremes? Well, it is clear from the text that knowing what locutionary act has been performed includes knowing what 'rhetic act' has been performed; and it is clear from the examples on p. 95 that specifying the rhetic act which has been performed includes more than merely specifying the *sense-and-reference*, in the restricted sense considered above, of what is said. For on that page the specification of the rhetic act is given by such descriptions as the following: He *told me to* get out; He *said he would* be there; He *asked whether* it was in Oxford or Cambridge.[6] So *if* knowing the locutionary *meaning* of what is said includes not simply knowing the minimal sense-and-reference content of what is said but also knowing what *rhetic act* has been performed, then we can always include in the locutionary meaning of what is said at least a *rough* classification of what is said under such general headings as, say, *declarative*, *imperative*, *interrogative*, and perhaps one or two more. This will take locutionary meaning well beyond restricted sense-and-reference while leaving it, in general, short of full illocutionary force.

But obvious queries arise about this interpretation, as so far described. *How much* more than restricted sense-and-reference is to be allowed into locutionary meaning by way of the specification of the rhetic act? *Which* of the linguistic devices employed are to be allowed to bear on the specification of the rhetic act, and why? Evidently, from the examples, the use of the imperative, the interrogative, or the indicative form is to be allowed to bear. Presumably also the optative—so that when the Dauphin in *Henry V* says 'Would it were day!' *his* rhetic act is to be described as: He expressed the wish that it was day. But if all these, what about others? What, in particular, of the case where an explicit performative formula is used? In what style should the rhetic act corresponding to an utterance of 'I promise to be there' be specified except in such a style as *He promised to be there*? What of the rhetic act corresponding to an utterance of 'I apologize'? And if the conventional force of the explicit performative formula is to be allowed, after all, to enter into locutionary meaning, why not also the conventional force of some of the other devices which Austin lists, such as certain

[6] My italics.

adverbs, adverbial phrases, and connecting particles? What, in general, is to stop this third interpretation, which was intended to be something intermediate between the extremes of the first and the second, from becoming indistinguishable from the first? What is to stop locutionary meaning from becoming indistinguishable from sense-*B*-meaning and hence including all that is included in sense-*A*-meaning?

In spite of these difficulties, however, I think we should not give up hope of finding an intermediate interpretation. I shall resume the attempt in the next section.

III

Even if it should turn out to be vain to press the question, what exactly is to be understood by 'locutionary meaning', it has not been vain to raise it, and to note the tensions in Austin's thinking which are revealed by raising it. Part of what is revealed is a certain ambivalence in Austin's attitude to a conception which, in one form or another, is really inescapable in philosophical, or broadly logical, theory. The conception I have in mind is that of the primary or essential bearers of truth-value, variously named, and no doubt variously conceived, as *statements, propositions, thoughts* (Frege), and *constatives* (Austin). 'The traditional statement', Austin says, 'is an abstraction, an ideal, and so is its traditional truth or falsity.'[7] A few lines later he characterizes the traditional conception of truth and falsity as an 'artificial abstraction which is always possible and legitimate for certain purposes'.[8] We are left a little uncertain as to whether the conception in question is an abstraction and none the worse for that, or whether it is an abstraction and a good deal the worse for that; whether it is an abstraction we have to make in the interests of a satisfactory general theory, or an abstraction which impedes the framing of a satisfactory general theory. We may incline to the former view of his views when we consider that one of the things we learn, or re-learn, from Austin is the need to distinguish and relate (i.e. not to muddle) different levels in the theory of language. Is not the theory of the proposition (or the theory of the constative) on one of these levels, interpenetrating with, but not to be confused with, the general theory

---

[7] Op. cit., p. 147.   [8] Op. cit., p. 148.

of linguistic meaning (sense A) and the general theory of communicated force, including illocutionary force (sense C)? And is not Austin's notion of locutionary meaning a gesture, though an unclear one, in this direction? But though these thoughts may incline us to suppose that he viewed the constative abstraction with some degree of favour, there is much to incline us to the opposite view of his views. There is, first, the symptomatic unclarity of his doctrine of locutionary meaning; and there are, secondly, the more direct indications of a certain grudgingness in his references to 'traditional' truth and falsity and their 'traditional' bearers. Some of the reasons advanced for this reserve I shall discuss in the next section. First (though this is by no means a matter to be wholly cleared up *en passant*) I shall say a little more about the abstraction in question by way of making a final attempt to relate it to the notion of locutionary meaning.

One thing, with cautious readiness, we can say at once. Any proposition is *capable* of being expressed either in some clause or sentence which is *capable*, in all linguistic propriety, of following the phrase 'it is true that' or in some logical compound (e.g. a disjunction) of such clauses or sentences. Let us call these clauses or sentences the 'normal forms' of expression of a proposition. And let us call the provision just laid down 'the normal-form provision'.

The normal-form provision leaves us uncommitted on a number of points. I mention some which are obviously relevant to any further attempt at interpreting the notion of locutionary meaning.

(i) First, a minor point. It is clear that at least for some interpretations (and those the more plausible) of this notion, those elements of the sense-A-meaning of what is said which are conventionally implied by such expressions as 'of course', 'therefore', 'nevertheless', etc., and (sometimes) 'fortunately', 'unhappily', etc. are not to be included in locutionary meaning. The same holds for the Fregean thought. Is this result guaranteed also for propositions by the normal-form provision? Not, I think, clearly. Consider such a clause as 'he is occupied', which is certainly capable of expressing a proposition. We have no clear guarantee that the introduction of the expression 'of course', which modifies the sense-A-meaning of what is said, would not thereby modify any proposition expressed. But I think we can add to our limited characterization to provide such a guarantee. The word-string 'He is happily occupied' can evidently be understood in two different ways; and this difference is identical with the difference between 'It is happily true that he is occupied' and 'It is true that he is happily occupied'. Perhaps, then, we can achieve the desired result by ruling that the only elements of sense-*A*-meaning which contribute to determining the content of the proposition expressed by a certain clause are those contributed by expressions which are such that, when 'it is true that' is prefixed to the clause, it would *not* be more felicitous to transfer the expressions in question from their original place in the clause to a place in the prefixed phrase. 'Of course', 'nevertheless', 'therefore', etc. in general fail to satisfy this requirement; 'It is true that he is of course married' or 'It is true that he is nevertheless married' are at best infelicitous shots at 'It is of course true that he's married' or 'It is nevertheless true that he's married'. We could indeed have 'It's true that he's therefore regretful' as well as 'It's therefore true that he's regretful'; but this serves only to emphasize the success of the ruling. The merit of the test lies not merely in its success but in its obvious relevance to the task in hand, i.e. that of delimiting what belongs to the proposition, the bearer of truth-value.

(ii) There is a more important matter on which the normal-form provision leaves us uncommitted. To say that propositions must be *capable* of being expressed in a certain form (the normal form) is really to say very little. It limits the notion of a proposition much less than it might appear to. It is not, by itself, to say either that a proposition is expressed only when that form is used or that a proposition is expressed only when one of a range of speech acts characteristically associated with that form is performed. It leaves quite open the question whether one and the same proposition, capable of expression in the normal form, may not also be capable of expression in forms associated with quite other speech acts. If we want a Fregean, or quasi-Fregean, limitation which will forbid us to say that 'Pay the bill now, John' (uttered as an instruction) may express a proposition, and the very same proposition as might be expressed by 'John is about to pay the bill' (uttered as a piece of information), then that limitation has yet to be imposed. The normal-form provision does not of itself give reason for denying that orders and instructions express propositions and indeed the same propositions as the corresponding predictions.

It is not difficult to find reasons for imposing a Fregean or quasi-Fregean limitation. One reason for such a limitation is this. Propositions, whatever they are, are supposed to be bearers of truth-value; but we should not ordinarily say that one who issues a command or instruction (say, 'Pay the bill now, John') had thereby said something true or false—true if the command was complied with, false if not. Now this might seem a superficial reason. But we can find a deeper reason behind it in the insight expressed by various philosophers,[9] into the difference in direction of 'match' or correspondence between the words and the world in the case of, say, assertions on the one hand and, say, commands on the other. A connected reason may be found in the view, held by many, that no 'logic of imperatives' (if there is anything deserving the name) can successfully be represented as strictly parallel to a 'logic of propositions'.[10] Now it is not my present purpose to say exactly what limitations on the notion of proposition are to be imposed. But I shall assume that *some* are to be imposed. And on this assumption, we may make another attempt at a scheme of interpretation for the notion of locutionary meaning.

But first let us note just one more point (iii) on which the normal-form provision leaves us uncommitted. I have already remarked that it does not commit us to the view that whenever a proposition is expressed, it is expressed in the normal form. Now I add that it does not commit us to the view that a clause having the normal form of a proposition always expresses the proposition which it would normally express if it were actually preceded by the words 'it is true that'. Thus, as far as the normal-form provision is concerned, it is open to us to hold (in what is surely an Austinian spirit) that, for example, the words 'I accuse the authorities of fabricating evidence' will usually, if uttered as a complete sentence, express the proposition which, in normal form, would be expressed by 'The authorities have fabricated

---

[9] See, for example, Miss Anscombe, *Intention*, § 32.

[10] This is controversial. See R. M. Hare, 'Some Alleged Differences between Imperatives and Indicatives', *Mind* (1967), for the contrary view.

evidence' and not the proposition which they would express if they were actually preceded by the words 'it is true that'; though they may *sometimes* express that proposition.

Now, then, to the scheme of interpretation. The proposal is, first, that in every case in which a locution as a whole expresses a proposition, we should say that its locutionary meaning is the proposition expressed. For such other broad classes of locutions as we may find it expedient to distinguish from proposition-expressing locutions, we shall need terms of art comparable with the term 'proposition', to set beside the latter. Let us suppose that 'imperative' is one such term, imperatives being variously expressible with the force of pieces of advice, requests, commands, recommendations, prayers, invitations, etc. Then, again, we should say, of every locution which, as a whole, expresses an imperative, that its locutionary meaning is the imperative expressed. As regards the elements of (restricted) 'sense-and-reference' they contain, imperative and proposition may sometimes be indistinguishable. But as locutionary meanings they are distinguished as proposition and imperative respectively. A scheme for separately specifying the illocutionary force and the locutionary meaning of single utterances which, as wholes, express propositions or imperatives (or any other broad classes we find it expedient to distinguish) might be imagined as follows:

X issues the____(that . . .) with the force of a *xxxxx*.

A specification of the general type of locutionary meaning fills the first blank, of specific locutionary content the second, of illocutionary force the third. Thus we might have such fillings as these:

$$X \text{ issues the} \begin{cases} (1) \text{ proposition } (that \text{ S } is \text{ P}) \\ (2) \text{ imperative } (that \text{ Z (person) } is \text{ to } \text{Y (act)}) \\ (3) \qquad\qquad ? \end{cases}$$

as a

with the force of a

by way of

$$\begin{cases} (1) \text{ accusation, report, forecast, conclusion, objection, hypothesis, guess, verdict, etc.} \\ (2) \text{ command, request, piece of advice, prayer, invitation, entreaty, etc.} \\ (3) \qquad\qquad ? \end{cases}$$

It would evidently be in harmony with a scheme of this kind, as also (it seems most likely) with Austin's intentions, to hold that the explicit performative formula, whether occurring as a part or as the whole of an utterance, has no locutionary meaning at all. But though in harmony with this scheme, such a position is not *demanded* by it. It would be perfectly consistent with the scheme to hold the quite contrary position that one who (seriously) utters an explicit performative of the form 'I *x* . . .' issues the *proposition* that he *x*s . . . with the force of an *x*-ing: e.g. to hold that someone who says 'I apologize' issues the proposition that he apologizes with the force of an apology; or that someone who says 'I warn you all that judgement is at hand' issues the proposition that he warns us all that judgement is at hand with the force of a warning. This position has gained popularity with philosophers recently, as against the position which Austin himself may be presumed to have favoured; and indeed it would be, in some respect, a simplification, though in others a complication. The scheme proposed is in itself neutral as between the two positions. In what follows in Part IV Section (3) I shall assume the Austinian position because it will simplify the presentation of the argument there, though it will make no difference to the principle of that argument.

Of course the above remarks are not offered as a complete characterization of the notion of a proposition; nor, patently, as a complete theory of the classification of speech acts. They do not even offer a decision-procedure for applying the partial classification proposed. They are intended only as *indications* of the place which the relatively abstract notions of proposition and imperative might be held to occupy on one possible form of interpretation, and that not the least plausible or attractive, of the notion of locutionary meaning. One minor modification of the *schema*, which it is worth making to forestall misunderstanding, is the following. On any view, propositions may be expressed by *parts* of utterances (e.g. co-ordinate or subordinate clauses or accusative and infinitive constructions), parts which are not themselves advanced with the force which belongs to the utterance as a whole; and it may be expedient to mark this point by replacing the term 'proposition' in the above *schema* with one less general. For this purpose Austin's own term 'constative' offers itself as a convenient candidate.

IV

Now, finally, I said I was going to mention some reasons which Austin might have had for viewing with a fairly cold eye the notion of the propositional abstraction, and hence for viewing with a fairly cold eye the proposal I have just made for the interpretation of the notion of locutionary meaning. I glanced at one of these reasons at the end of my consideration of Interpretation II: but it is worth considering at greater length, as I shall do in section (3) below.

It is not immediately obvious how far Austin's position on this matter actually suffered change. In his 1950 paper, 'Truth', he regarded with sufficient favour the notion of the primary and fundamental bearer of truth-value to think it worthwhile to inquire into the name and nature of 'that which at bottom we are always saying "is true"';[11] and then to advance, though with reservations, the theory that the predicate 'is true' stands for a certain 'rather boring yet satisfactory relation' which may sometimes hold 'between words and world'.[12] In *How to Do Things with Words* the note of reservation sounds more strongly: 'truth and falsity (except by an artificial abstraction which is always possible and legitimate for certain purposes) are not names for relations, qualities, or whatnot, but for a dimension of assessment.'[13] The exceptive clause allows us to suppose that there has been no fundamental change of position, even though reserve may have deepened into coldness. Let us look at the reasons for this reserve. We shall see that none of them is a good reason.

(1) One of them seems to concern the word 'statement', Austin's preferred name (in 1950) for that of which 'at bottom' we predicate 'is true'. That he should have had reservations about the *name* is surely natural enough. For, as he frequently points out, the verb 'to state' and the noun 'statement' are naturally used only in a relatively confined class of cases.[14] There are many other cases to which this term is not naturally

---

[11] *Philosophical Papers*, p. 86; 2nd edn., p. 118.

[12] Op. cit., p. 107. About this theory I have already had my say, or more than my say, and I shall not repeat criticisms already made.

[13] *How to Do Things with Words*, p. 148. See also p. 144.

[14] See *How to Do Things with Words*, pp. 137, 146, etc., also *Philosophical Papers* pp. 236-7.

applied, but in which the uninhibited theorist of the constative would say that a constative is issued; and yet many more, as already remarked, where the uninhibited theorist of the proposition would say that a proposition is expressed, though not 'constated' (issued as a constative).

It scarcely seems, however, that we have, in these points about the term 'statement', a reason for scepticism about the theory of propositions. We might take these points, rather, as reasons for viewing with favour the employment of the artificial term, 'proposition', instead of the common word, 'statement'. It is easy to meet, if it should be issued, the challenge to explain why we do not have in common use an expression with just the coverage which the artificial term is intended to have. For we do not commonly talk about propositions in general, and we do not commonly talk about particular propositions except when they come before us as what somebody does or might believe, suppose, assert, declare, guess, surmise, hypothesize, premise, conclude, imply, etc. We have a correspondingly rich range of substantival expressions for referring to propositions under the guises under which they come before us; and there is no reason why we should, in actual situations, feel the need for a term which abstracts from any and every such guise, especially when we also have at our disposal a standard and neutral form (the 'that'-clause) for specifying the *content* of any particular belief, hypothesis, conclusion, etc. The challenge to be thus met is in any case scarcely one which Austin would be in a position to issue. Given the freedom with which technical terms proliferate in *How to Do Things with Words*, Austin could scarcely think it a reproach to any theorist that he should feel the need of a classification not commonly made in the daily business of communication.

(2) A class of reasons for regarding the 'traditional' conception of *truth* as undesirably abstract is introduced by way of two examples of rather rough-and-ready geographical and historical description, viz. 'France is hexagonal' and 'Lord Raglan won the battle of Alma'.[15] Some of Austin's comments on these remarks are plainly correct. He points out that, like many others, they may be adequate for some purposes and not for others, suitable to some contexts and not to others. But this

[15] *How to Do Things with Words*, pp. 142–3.

tolerance wavers when the words 'true' and 'false' come into play. 'How can one answer this question', he says, 'whether it's true or false that France is hexagonal? It is just rough, and that is the right and final answer to the question of the relation of "France is hexagonal" to France. It is a rough description; it is not a true or a false one.' But why should Austin refuse 'true' and 'false' a place even in a right and final answer? Couldn't we say 'It's roughly true that France is hexagonal'? (It's not even roughly true, it's completely false, that France has the shape of a trapezium.) Couldn't we also say 'It's true (*sans phrase*) that France is roughly hexagonal'? Austin successfully makes us aware of the hesitation we feel when confronted with the hold-up question 'Is it true or false that France is hexagonal?' But it is not so much the presence of the words 'true' and 'false' as the absence of qualification or context that accounts for the hesitation. We should feel just the same hesitation over 'Is France hexagonal or isn't it?'

This comes out clearly enough in his own presentation of his second example. He asks: 'Did Lord Raglan then win the battle of Alma or did he not?' It seems in this case that the 'pointlessness' of insisting on the statement's truth or falsity is the same thing as the pointlessness of insisting that either he did or he didn't. Austin's own positive comment on this case has a measure of oddity. 'Lord Raglan won the battle of Alma' is, he says, not true or false, but exaggerated, an exaggeration. But wouldn't it really be something like a mild witticism to say that it was an *exaggeration* to say that Lord Raglan won the battle of Alma?

It is by no means an easy matter to see exactly what Austin took the import of such examples to be. Of course there are descriptions which are adequate in some contexts and not in others; of course, too, there are descriptions which are sometimes only more or less apt for the situations we are inclined or half-inclined to apply them to. Is it Austin's point that the words 'true' and 'false' are *never* in place in such cases? But this seems to be not strictly (or not at all) true. If we are happily operating at a level, in a context, at or in which descriptions which, from another point of view might be regarded as oversimplified, are perfectly adequate, then it may be perfectly all right to employ the words 'true' and 'false' without qualification. If we are operating at a more critical level—or dealing with descriptions which, at any level, are only more or less apt for the particular situation in question—we have at our disposal expressions which, or some of which, can be used *either* to modify the descriptive predicates themselves *or* to modify the predicate 'true'. I have in mind such expressions as 'roughly', 'more or less', 'not strictly', 'not exactly', 'not altogether', and so on.

Indeed Austin might have found in this last point some prima facie support for his own (1950) theory of truth. When we say such things as 'He's not exactly drunk', 'He's not strictly speaking a relation', 'It's only approximately square', we might, with some justice, in some cases, say that we are talking both about the words and the world, both about the situation and the description. In so far as we can make remarks equivalent to these, employing the word 'true', we have, to an equivalent degree, remarks about the relation of words to world. But of course it is well for a defender of the Austinian theory of truth *not* to make *this* point. To gain it would be to lose the match. To admit it is to admit the wooden horse. For the point is that the presence or absence of the word 'true' *makes no difference* in this respect.

Perhaps, however, the point of Austin's examples is simply to bring out the illusoriness of a certain concept of truth. According to this conception, the predicate 'is true' is one which in the case of *every* constative utterance (or *every* propositional part of an utterance), either holds absolutely and without qualification or absolutely and without qualification fails to hold. That this is an illusory conception very few theorists of the proposition would have difficulty in agreeing; but they need not agree that it is, or ever was, *their* conception.

(3) Austin's third reason for coldness about the propositional abstraction is of a rather different kind from those so far considered. His point is, or seems to be, to put it in the very terms he would regard it as a reason for questioning—that just as the facts of the case bear on the truth or falsity of a constative, so the facts of the case bear on the warrantedness or unwarrantedness of an imperative.[16] The facts of the case may be such as to make a request a reasonable request, an order a sound or justified order, a piece of advice good advice; or they may be such that the request is unreasonable, the order unsound, the

[16] See pp. 141, 144.

advice bad. (Of course, all these assessments are liable to qualifications of degree, of more or less.) If the salt is nearer to you
than it is to me, it may be reasonable of me to ask you to pass it.
If it is nearer to me than to you, it may not be. If you are a good
runner and a bad shot, my advice to you to run rather than stay
and shoot may be good advice and the advice to stay and shoot
rather than run may be bad advice. The strategic situation may
be such as to justify the order to stand or it may be such as to
justify the order to retreat. And so on.

All this is evidently correct. But Austin invites us to regard it
as a reason for *assimilating* this kind of assessment of requests,
advice, commands, etc. to the kind of assessment which we
make of constatives when we declare them true or false. When
he says that 'true' and 'false' are the names of a general dimension of assessment, he means to include *both* the above kinds of
assessment in this general dimension. He wants us to join him
in refusing to draw any sharp line between saying that an
announcement, accusation, or surmise was true, and saying that
a request, a piece of advice, or a command was warranted or
justified by the facts of the case.[17]

It will be clear why I say that this third point of Austin is in
a different class from the preceding two. The theorist of the
proposition can accept with equanimity, and even welcome,
much that is just in the first two points. But he must reject the
assimilation proposed in the third. If he is impressed by an
analogy between constatives and imperatives, it will be by a
different analogy. He will be impressed by the fact that just as
constatives are (just or more or less) true or not, so imperatives
are (just or more or less) complied with or not. He may even be
prepared to assimilate them to each other (for some purposes)
on this ground, the ground, we might say, of the possibility of
common content. But of course this ground of assimilation is
totally different from that proposed by Austin.

But is the theorist of the proposition justified as against
Austin? Surely he is. And surely Austin goes against his own
best insights in suggesting he is not. Let us call the assessment

---

[17] Let me recall that in what follows I ignore the un-Austinian option, left open
by the scheme of the final interpretation, of regarding explicit performatives as,
without exception, constatives. This merely simplifies the statement of the ensuing criticisms. It makes no difference of principle.

of a piece of advice, an order, or a request, etc. as sound or unsound, reasonable or unreasonable etc., its warrantability-valuation, and let us call the assessment of an (undoubted) constative as (just or more or less) true or false its truth-valuation. What Austin proposes is that we regard warrantability-valuation and truth-valuation as belonging to a single dimension of assessment—for which he appropriates the name, 'the truth-and-falsity dimension'. Let us instead call this supposed single dimension of assessment the dimension of S-valuation ('S' for 'satisfactoriness') and distinguish throughout between positive and negative S-valuation.

Now Austin himself has insisted on distinguishing the locutionary meaning of an utterance from all its other aspects. Disregarding the first interpretation of 'locutionary meaning', which is certainly un-Austinian, we have the choice of regarding locutionary meanings as differentiated into broad classes of which the constative and the imperative are two (the final interpretation); or of regarding locutionary meanings as undifferentiated throughout (the second interpretation). But whichever of these choices we make, we cannot possibly regard locutionary meanings as related in a homogeneous manner to conditions for positive S-valuation throughout the field of this supposed single dimension of assessment. If we take constatives as forming one broad class of locutionary meanings, and imperatives another, we must note that to specify constative locutionary meanings is the same thing as to specify conditions for positive S-valuation, whereas to specify imperative locutionary meanings is not even to begin to specify conditions for positive S-valuation; it is simply to say who, according to the imperative, is to do what. If, on the other hand, we are not to regard locutionary meanings as thus broadly differentiated, then we must note that in every case the specification of locutionary meaning is a specification of a possible state of affairs; and, once we are informed of the type of speech act involved, we can scarcely fail to note a distinction between cases in which the obtaining or coming to obtain of that state of affairs would constitute the satisfaction of conditions for positive S-valuation (the constative cases) and cases in which the obtaining or coming to obtain of that state of affairs would be quite irrelevant to positive S-valuation (the imperative cases).

These are surely sufficient reasons for re-affirming a clear distinction between truth-valuation and warrantability-valuation. Moreover they are reasons to which we are invited to attend by Austin's own distinction between locutionary meaning and illocutionary force. We need not, of course, deny that truth-valuation and warrantability-valuation have something in common, nor that the grounds for both may, in particular cases, be as close as you please: for example, the fact that it is raining may in one way justify my assertion that it is raining and in another way may justify my urging you to take an umbrella. But we cannot, surely, find it felicitous to mark these points by appropriating the names 'truth' and 'falsity' in the way Austin suggests.

V

Some Types of Performative Utterance

I BELIEVE that the notion, so paradigmatically Austin's, of performative utterances, has proved fertile—as philosophical notions sometimes do—at least in part because of its provoking instability. It has shown a persistent tendency, as of course Austin himself found, both to wobble and to ramify when subjected to close scrutiny, and thus can fruitfully lead one into, not just one topic, but several. I think also, however, that this tendency to waver has, not at all surprisingly, bred certain confusions (in myself among others); and if these are not to become chronic, distinctions should be attempted. In this paper I offer some distinctions and kindred considerations, by no means all of them novel.

I

Let us begin with what was, I suppose, quite clearly the basic thought that gave rise to the notion of performative utterances —namely, the thought, simple enough in formulation though less so in content, that sometimes to *say* something is to *do* something. Two points at once call for attention here.

First, it is to be noticed that this basic thought is—and, historically, was—that *sometimes* saying is doing. It is clear enough that Austin, however his thoughts may have gone at later stages, had at first the idea that performative utterances were to be a special case; the term was meant to pick out some sub-class of utterances, which were then to be contrasted with others which were not performative. We have to consider, then, first, whether, and if so when and why, to say something

is to do something, in a sense, if there is one, in which to say
something is not necessarily, or absolutely always, or even
normally, to do something, but is so only sometimes, in special
cases.

Second, it is to be noticed that, in this basic thought, no
particular restriction is indicated on the *kinds* of doings that
sayings sometimes are—except, of course, that they are to be
kinds of doings which can be done by saying something. There
is, in particular and importantly, no restriction here to the kind
or kinds of doings which came later to be called, vaguely
enough, 'speech acts'. It seems in fact to be a plain consequence
of the foregoing point that this must be so; for if, as came later
to be held by many, to issue an utterance is always, even perhaps
necessarily, to perform some speech act or acts, we are obviously
not going to pick out, by reference to doings of *that* sort, a *sub-
class* of utterances to issue which is to do something. In any case
it seems clear from Austin's own early examples that he was
not at first thinking particularly, or even at all, of (as one might
say, Searlean) *linguistic* acts;[1] some of his early examples are, for
instance, of legal doings, such as getting married or bequeathing
property; he also mentioned at an early stage such performances
as betting, naming ships, and baptizing people or penguins. In
all this he was clearly thinking in fact, or was perfectly prepared
to think, of any sorts of doings at all in the doing of which
certain utterances figured as what he at times called, borrowing
from lawyers, the 'operative' element.[2]

The question is, then, at this stage, how utterances are sometimes 'operative'—how it is, as one might put it, that one who
issues an utterance thereby sometimes does something, *over and
above* whatever it may be (and we are not yet going into this)
that he necessarily does just as a speaker of the language, merely
in saying whatever it is that he says. Well, the answer that Austin
first gave to this question is one that indeed very naturally
suggests itself; namely, sometimes there exist rules, or legal
provisions, or more or less commonly or officially recognized
practices—let us say broadly, as he usually did, *conventions*—
which provide that saying something or other is to be, is to

---

[1] The allusion is, of course, to John Searle's *Speech Acts* (1969).
[2] e.g. in 'Performative Utterances', *Philosophical Papers* (1961), p. 223; (2nd edn.,
1970,) p. 236.

constitute or count as, doing whatever it may be.[3] There is, familiarly enough, a large class of doings, well exemplified by but of course not confined to legal doings or certain doings in the playing of games, which could be said essentially to *consist in* the exploitation or following or invoking of certain conventions; in a sub-class of such cases, exploiting or following or invoking the relevant conventions involves, sometimes mandatorily, the saying of certain words; and in those cases, saying the words is, counts as, in virtue of the convention, doing the thing. This seems to me pretty clearly to be the most conspicuous idea discernible in Austin's earlier remarks on this topic—the idea, that is, of utterances which are performative, to issue which is to do something, in virtue of *conventions* to the effect that to say those things counts as, or constitutes, doing whatever it may be: as to say 'Three no trumps', for example, can constitute bidding, an operation defined (as one might say) by the rules of bridge. Four comments on this.

First, it seems clear that, whatever Austin himself or others may subsequently have come to think, there is nothing whatever wrong with this idea. No doubt, like many other ideas, it is a bit fuzzy at the edges. (Austin was well aware of that.) When we have said that we are concerned here with conventions in virtue of which to say so-and-so constitutes doing such-and-such, we shall certainly find, for instance, that we are not always quite sure what is, or whether there is, a convention in the appropriate sense; we shall sometimes ask, for instance, and be perplexed in answering, the question whether there is a *convention* that to say *X counts as* doing *Y*, or whether perhaps it is merely *customary*, or usual, that one who says *X* would *be taken* to be doing *Y*. The notion of a convention, that is, is not absolutely hard-edged, especially perhaps in the slightly stretched sense that the term is here being given. Also, and importantly, as already hinted, if *this* notion of performative utterance is to identify a *sub-class* of utterances, we shall of course have to rope off the conventions we are concerned with at this stage from those which (as some would say) essentially enter into all linguistic utterance merely as such; for if conventions are exploited in simply saying anything at all, it will have to be in

---

[3] e.g. *How to Do Things with Words*, p. 14; 'Performative Utterances', p. 224; 2nd edn., p. 237.

virtue of conventions of sorts distinguishable from those that to say is only *sometimes* to do. But these snags are not fatal. There are clear cases, though also penumbral ones, of conventions; there are conventions which, while involving utterance, are clearly not *linguistic* conventions—not, as one might put it, parts of the *language*; and if so, there is an at any rate decently discriminable species of utterances such that, in virtue of conventions that are not linguistic, to issue such utterances is, counts as, constitutes, doing this or that.

Second, if one has *this* notion of performative utterance, it is clearly reasonable and right to investigate, as Austin did early and extensively, the topic of what he called 'infelicity'. For if it is to be by convention that to say X constitutes doing Y, it will be illuminating to consider why, and in how many sorts of ways, saying X sometimes doesn't quite, or even at all, amount to doing Y—why, and in how many sorts of ways, the purported doing may not happily 'come off'. What is involved in doing it properly will be illuminated by considering how things may go wrong. For of course, in these cases, doing is never *just* saying: it is saying 'happily'—saying, that is, in the absence of the sorts of things that Austin called misfires and abuses—misapplications, flaws, hitches, insincerities, and what not. Where there is a convention that to do (e.g. say) X counts as doing Y, Y will only actually get done if X is done (e.g. said) by the right person, at the right time and place, in the right way, and so on.

Third, it is again clearly right to say here, as Austin did, that one who issues a performative utterance in *this* sense does not commonly, in his utterance, state *that* he is doing what he is therein doing. In saying 'Three no trumps' I bid, but I do not state that I am bidding; in saying 'How's that?' (in cricket) I appeal, but I do not state that I am appealing; and so on. Austin held, I think, that one who, in saying X, does Y in fact *never* therein states that he is doing Y; this is highly arguable, and I argue it later; but it is certainly true and even obvious that he doesn't necessarily.

Fourth, if, as we have said, there is at this point no particular restriction on the kinds of doings that sayings sometimes are—except, of course, that they should be capable of being done, in virtue of suitable conventions, by saying something—it is equally clear, though far more commonly overlooked, that there can be at this point no restriction either on the kinds of sayings that can be doings. If our idea is, as I think it clear that Austin's idea originally was, that of sayings which, in virtue of conventions, constitute doings, it should be perfectly clear that sayings of any linguistic form or sort at all could figure in this role; it is simply a matter of laying down, or of there being, the relevant conventions. Like 'Three no trumps', such sayings need not be sentences; they need not even consist of (in any *other* connection) meaningful words of any language; but where sentences are uttered, they may be indicative, interrogative, imperative, active or passive, and so on and so on. Two points in particular. A saying which, by convention, counts as doing something could perfectly well be the saying of something true or false (though indeed, in such a case, truth or falsehood might not be the point mainly at issue)—so that the happy–unhappy distinction does not in any way *exclude* the true–false distinction (though of course it differs from it);[4] and secondly, while Austin's own early examples happened to be mostly of the 'I *X*' form—in the non-continuous present tense, first person indicative active— there is actually no reason why performative utterances, in this sense, *should* be in, or even be capable of being put into, that form in particular. There is, as we shall see, something special about that form, but not in this connection; for it is really obvious that any sort of saying whatever—even an otherwise perfectly senseless one—could in principle, were there to exist the appropriate convention, count as or constitute doing something. For of course what distinguishes performative utterances in *this* sense is not that, grammatically or whatever, they are a special sort of saying, but that, whatever sort of saying they may be, there are conventions in virtue of which that saying counts as doing. The distinguishing feature is extra-linguistic. It is accordingly not surprising that, when Austin raised the question of a 'grammatical' criterion for performativeness,[5] he found that

---

[4] Austin says at first that performative utterances are 'not true or false' (e.g. 'Performative Utterances', p. 222; 2nd edn., p. 235; and *How to Do Things with Words*, p. 5), and even seems at times to take that as a partial criterion of performativeness. He qualifies this later—'Considerations of the type of truth and falsity may infect performatives (or some performatives)' (*How to Do Things with Words*, p. 55)—not, however, as a glance at his text will show, for anything like the reason I have in mind here.

[5] *How to Do Things with Words*, pp. 55 ff.

there was not one; what needs explaining is why he should even have toyed with the idea that there might be, and that I shall return to.

To sum up this first section, then: it seems to me that we have here a notion of performative utterance that is, or at least would be capable of being made, quite decently clear. We assume the existence of languages that people speak, in which all sorts of things, on all sorts of topics, can be said. We observe that there are, in law and in games but in many other cases too, things that people do that essentially consist in, or are constituted by, the exploitation or invocation of certain conventions (other than those, if they are such, involved in merely speaking the language); and we observe further that, in some of these cases, exploiting or invoking the relevant conventions crucially consists in, or includes, the uttering of certain words. We can then say with clear sense that, in such cases, one who issues the relevant utterance not merely *says* something (as in any standard instance of speaking the language), but further, in virtue of the applicable convention, thereby (of course if things otherwise go happily) *does* something; and we call the sub-class of utterances of which this is true *performative* utterances. What we have thus got is not, we observe, a special sort of sentences, or anything in any way distinguishable on purely linguistic grounds; what we have is a class of utterances, linguistically quite heterogeneous, which have in common that, in virtue of non-linguistic conventions, to issue them (happily) *counts* as *doing* this or that. As such they are, of course, a sub-class not only of utterances, but also of what might be called conventionally-significant doings, many of which will differ in not involving utterance at all.

II

To launch our second stage, let us bring up again the basic thought that sometimes to *say* something is to *do* something. We have considered and sketched one way in which this might be taken—in which it would be true that some utterances, but not all, are 'performative'; namely, some utterance sometimes plays a crucial, indeed 'operative' role in the execution of convention-constituted doings or procedures. But of course one might move from that basic thought in a very different direction. For surely, one might say, to say something is, not sometimes, but absolutely always, to do something; and this, I take it, though as vague as could be, is undoubtedly in some sense true. There is a sense, then, one might wish to say, in which *all* utterances are performative; that is, whenever anyone says anything, there is always *something* that he therein does. And thus there comes in the whole topic of what came to be called 'speech acts'—of those things that are done, not now just sometimes, but standardly, even always, even necessarily perhaps, in standardly issuing any utterance in a language at all.

Now this topic of speech acts—which is indeed, if not inexhaustible, at any rate very, very far from being exhausted—is not one that I mean to embark upon on this occasion. I want to say in this connection only four brief things.

The first is that, if it is true, as I presume it is, that to say something is always, in a considerable diversity of ways and senses, to do something—so that in that sense, if we choose to say so, all utterance is performative—it obviously does not follow that we were wrong before; it does not follow that the previously-sketched class of what we might call Mark I performative utterances was in any way a bogus class, or that there was anything amiss in our distinction of those utterances from others. There is nothing that this new thought, so to speak, requires us to give up; we are simply moving on to something else. For no doubt it is the case that to say, for instance, 'What's the date today?' or 'The train leaves at three', is to do something—various things indeed; but to say those things is not, ordinarily anyway, to do something in virtue of, or as an element in, some non-linguistic conventional procedure, in at all the way in which to say 'Three no trumps', in playing bridge, is to make a bid. Thus to observe that there is, and to embark on the investigation of, the general topic of the things speakers standardly do in speaking has no tendency at all to show that the foregoing attempt to isolate a *sub-class* of performative utterances has 'broken down';[6] we may think we have moved

---

[6] Austin himself says at times that 'in its original form' the distinction 'breaks down' (e.g. 'Performative Utterances', p. 238; 2nd edn., p. 251; see also *How to Do Things with Words*, p. 149). He had in mind here both that 'stating' is in a way doing, and that 'something like' truth and falsity can 'infect' performatives. However, if the 'original' distinction is made to rest on the presence or absence of

on from that to something more general and interesting, but we have also moved on to something quite different; for even if all speaking is—in one way or another—doing, it will still be only sometimes that to say is—in virtue of special, non-linguistic conventions—to do.

The second point is this. When we switch our attention from the first idea of a special sub-class of performative utterances to the investigation of what is done in speaking merely as such , we should be careful not to carry over to this latter topic notions that are valid only for the former one. Austin, I think, went a bit wrong here. It was a feature—it was, in fact, the defining feature—of performative utterances in the first sense that it was *by convention* that, in those cases, to say was to do; to say 'Three no trumps' was to bid because, and only because, there was a rule (convention) of the game being played in virtue of which such an utterance counted in appropriate circumstances as bidding. Austin, I believe, was apt to take for granted that the same was to be said of his later interest, speech acts in general— these also were to be, in general, conventional or convention-constituted acts.[7] But this surely is not true in general. It may be that one who issues the utterance 'The train leaves at three' therein says that the train leaves at three because, and only because, there are conventions of English which assign that sense to that sentence (it *may* be); but if, in saying 'The train leaves at three', I am warning you not to dilly-dally over your lunch, there is no *convention* which *makes* my utterance an act of warning, or of issuing *that* warning; it is an act of warning if I spoke with the intention of alerting you to some putative peril, in this case the possible peril of missing your train. This is true, I think, in general, though not without exception, of illocutionary forces; they are not in general convention-constituted— which is perhaps exactly why they can and should be, for most utterances anyway, distinguished from *meanings*. The idea that linguistic doings are somehow *all* 'conventional' is an improper hangover, I think, from the original idea of the Mark I kind of (by definition) convention-dependent performative utterance.[8]

---

conventions in virtue of which certain utterances *count as* doing this or that, it does not break down at all, for those or any other reasons.

  [7] e.g. *How to Do Things with Words*, p. 105, and several other passages also.
  [8] Cf. Strawson, 'Intention and Convention in Speech Acts', first published in

My third and fourth points are almost too obvious to be worth mentioning, but let me not shrink from mentioning them all the same. They are that, if we move on to consider ways and senses in which to say is standardly, even always, to do, and if in that sense we see fit to say that all utterance is performative, it will be even more obvious than it was before that performative utterance does not stand in contrast with or exclude—for of course it will often simply *be*—the saying of something true or false; and it will also be even more obvious than it was before that one who, in speaking, does such-and-such does not necessarily, or even normally, state *that* he is doing it *in* what he says. If to speak is, in general, to perform speech acts, then obviously to say, truly or falsely, 'This train stops at Reading' is to perform speech acts; and if, in saying 'This train stops at Reading', I am, say, giving you information, I do not therein state *that* I am doing so, or *that* I am doing anything else either.

III

I come now to my third stage, which is less drably uncontroversial and, I hope, more interesting. We have just said, fearlessly stating the obvious, that, it being presumably true in some sense that a speaker who says anything at all therein does *something*, it is not necessarily true, or even often so, that in what he says he says *that* he is doing what he is doing (I can warn or advise or rebuke you, and so on, without saying *that* I do); and we may now add to this the observation that, when speakers speak, there will often be, not only no explicit *statement*, but nothing at all in the words themselves, which explicitly signals what speakers are doing in saying them—or it might be better to put that the other way round: when speakers speak, there will normally be at any rate some things they therein do the doing of which is not explicitly signalled in any way in the words they utter. But then our eye may be caught by another special case here—the case of what Austin came to call *explicit* performatives. Well, how do these fit in?

Now the particular case that I want to say something about here is that common and quite familiar one in which the word

Philosophical Review (October 1964), pp. 439–60), also in his *Logico-Linguistic Papers*, pp. 149–69.

for what (or rather, for one thing which) the speaker could be
said to be doing in speaking actually enters as the main verb
in the sentence he utters—where, in promising, he says 'I
promise', in advising, 'I advise you to . . .', and so on. This is
not, of course, as Austin often reminds us, the only way in which
what the speaker is up to can be explicitly indicated in what he
says; for—stretching 'speaker' and 'says' a little—we have for
instance the cases of the notice reading 'Please keep car windows
closed' with WARNING above, or of the sentence, 'Gas-
capes will be worn' on a sheet of paper headed 'Part II Orders';
where it is, I suppose, made explicit that those sentences,
respectively imperative and future-tense indicative, are to be
taken respectively as issuings of a warning and an order. However, the case in which the word for what the speaker is doing
appears, in the first person, as the verb in the sentence he utters
has features of special interest, and that is the case that I want to
go on about.

The first issue is this. We have here a special class of utterances
—the special case in which, as does not usually occur, the
speaker explicitly indicates something that he is doing in speaking by incorporating the word *for* what he is doing *in* what he
says. Now, is this the *same* special case as that of Mark I performative utterance—the case of 'operative' utterance as
roughed out in my first section above? I regret to say that
something of this sort has certainly, very sloppily, been supposed; it has been thought, that is, that, starting out with the
basic idea that to say is sometimes to do, and going on to reflect
that to say, after all, is always to do *something*, we can then be
led back, so to speak, to our original notion of a *special* case by
observing that there really is that special case in which what is
done is explicitly indicated *in* the utterance. Though it pains me
to mention this, I myself once wrote as follows:

Austin supposed at first that such [i.e. performative] utterances were
a special case—that these cases, in which to say something was to do
something, to 'perform an act', could be contrasted with more
ordinary cases of simple saying. But later, in the course of trying to
make this contrast clearer and sharper, he came to realize that, while
his original performative utterances were indeed a special case, they
were not special quite in the way that he had supposed. It was not
that, in those cases, to say something was to do something, for this,

he now held, was true of every case . . . The difference is that, in the cases he had at first considered, it is made *explicit* in the utterance what speech act it is that the speaker is performing. This indeed is a special feature of certain utterances . . .[9]

I regret to say, however, that this, though it seems to run quite smoothly and would be, historically, pleasingly neat if it were correct, is actually completely wrong; the train of thought sketched, that is, is a muddled and mistaken one.

It is really perfectly obvious that this is so; we have here two quite different special cases, in no sense one and the same one. For one thing, while the examples with which Austin introduced the notion of performative utterance were mostly (which I suppose is what misleads one) of the explicit performative kind, it is just not true that all were—he cites, for instance, the 'operative' words in the ceremony of marriage, which, whatever they may be, are certainly not 'I marry . . .' Again, there is really, as I have noted above, no suggestion at that early stage that the doings that sayings sometimes are are to be '*speech* acts'. But above all what Austin says at that stage *about* performative utterances plainly does not require that they *should* be of the explicit performative form, even if it so happened that a lot of his examples were—for if the Mark I idea is, as I think it clearly was, that of utterance which, in virtue of some appropriate convention, counts as or constitutes doing such-and-such, then there is, as we have noted, plainly no restriction whatever on what shape or form such utterances might have, and in particular no reason why they *should* be of the form 'I *X*', where '*X*-ing' is the word for what the speaker does. The idea of saying something which, by convention, counts as doing such-and-such, and the idea of saying something in which the *words* make explicit in a particular way *what* one is doing, are really completely different ideas; the classes of utterances they pick out are not even extensionally equivalent; and therefore I was, of course, completely wrong in representing the notion of the explicit performative formula as some kind of re-instatement, or more sophisticated version, of the original notion. But if I got this point wrong, I do not think Austin himself was perfectly clear about it; for he raises at an early stage, as I have already mentioned,

---

[9] *English Philosophy since 1900* (2nd edn., 1969), p. 104.

the question whether there is a reliable formal, or as he puts it 'grammatical', way of identifying Mark I performative utterances; and although he comes correctly to the conclusion that there is not, he does not say explicitly, as I think he could and should have done, that there is absolutely no reason to think that there might have been. The notion he thought at any rate worth examining—that performative utterances might be those that were either already in, or could readily be put into, the 'I *X*' form, in saying which the speaker *X*-es—is one that, I think, would not have struck him as even plausible if he had quite clearly seen that what he later called explicit performatives were *quite* different creatures from the Mark I variety, 'operative' utterances in convention-constituted procedures.[10] For whereas it is of course the distinctive 'formal' mark of these explicit performatives that the word for what the speaker is doing puts in a special sort of appearance in the sentence he utters, there is absolutely no reason why the operative words in some conventional procedure *should* include the *word for* what is, by convention, done in their (felicitous) utterance. There is no reason why the conventional formulae for bidding (in bridge) should have to incorporate the word 'bid', or for appealing (in cricket) to incorporate the word 'appeal'; such formulae can, as we have seen, be of any verbal form at all, and there could not possibly be a *formal* way of picking them out.

Next, I want to put forward the proposition that latter-day explicit performatives are, not only not identical or co-extensive with Mark I performative utterances, but actually far more unlike them, and far more like what we may vaguely call 'ordinary' utterances, than has, to my knowledge, been supposed hitherto.[11]

---

[10] What makes the task of the historical disentangler a rather difficult one here is that Austin in fact—and in *How to Do Things with Words*, fully overtly—introduced the idea of performatives in a 'provisional' way, but did not subsequently consider in any great detail how much of the provisional account was to be conceived of as surviving. It was thus possible to think, as I did, that the 'provisional' performative turned out to survive, after refinement, *as* the *explicit* performative; and it is not, I think, certain that Austin did not think so too, though I hope he did not.

[11] When I first wrote what follows, in 1970, I had the feeling of going riskily out on an otherwise unoccupied limb. I had come across something close to what I wished to say in Stephen Schiffer's thesis *Meaning* (then unpublished); but he, perhaps rightly of course, did not go quite so far. Later, however, David Wiggins brought to my notice his own claim that explicit performatives can be taken as 'straightforward statements', in a then unpublished piece called 'On sentence-

Consider the Mark I performative utterance 'Three no trumps', as issued appropriately by a speaker engaged in playing bridge. We can agree, I take it, that he therein bids; that it is in virtue of a rule or convention of the game being played that he therein bids; but that, though he bids, he does not in what he says say *that* he bids, or (in this case) say anything at all that is true or false. Now much of this was held by Austin, and has been held more or less unquestioningly by many others, to be true also of explicit performatives, of the 'I *X*' species of utterance in issuing which the speaker *X*-es. This is why Austin said that such utterances were 'masqueraders';[12] being in the first person present indicative active, they look like, one might almost say they pose as, autobiographical *statements* by the speaker about himself, whereas in fact, he held, one who says, for example, 'I promise' does not say *that* he promises, or anything else that could be true or false—he just *promises*, and he does so, moreover, in virtue of a convention. But I now want to suggest that there is actually no need to look at it in this way at all—that explicit performative utterances are *not* masqueraders, that they are to be construed exactly as their form or 'grammar' suggests that they should be, and that conventions do not (necessarily anyway) come in at all here. Austin was at pains to distinguish making it explicit that one is doing something, from saying that one does it; in explicitly performative utterance, he held, the speaker does not say *that* he, for instance, advises, but merely makes it explicitly clear that he does so. I want to suggest that this is not so—that in saying, for example, 'I advise you to resign', I do indeed make it explicitly clear that I am offering you advice, but that I do so just by saying, truly or falsely, that I do. It seems clear that this suggestion, if one can make it stand up, would be theoretically to be much welcomed, as much simplifying any general doctrine of the indicative mood. The class of explicit performatives, that is, would not have to appear as an exception, or anomaly, to the tidy principle that one who says 'I *X*' therein says that he *X*-es, but as a perfectly regular, standard use of the first person present indicative active. For

---

sense, word-sense and difference of word-sense', which was to appear in *Semantics*, edd. Jacobovits and Steinberg; and he mentioned other allies. See also a tentative footnote in my *The Object of Morality*, p. 107.

[12] e.g. *How to Do Things with Words*, p. 4.

that reason, one would *like* what I am about to propound to be correct; but is it?

Well, some, I dare say, will think it just *obvious* that it is wrong; they may find it just obvious, as apparently Austin did, and as I myself did for years and years, that 'I promise', said in promising, is not true or false, and in particular that one who so says 'I promise' does not say that he promises. But what arguments are there, in fact, against the contrary view?

One, I suppose, might go like this. What I am suggesting is, in effect, that explicit performatives are to be construed as perfectly *ordinary* first person present indicatives. Now one who produces an undoubted sentence of that sort, the sentence, for instance, 'I smoke', undoubtedly says therein that he smokes; and what he so says of himself is either true or false; but of course for him to say that he smokes, and even to say truly that he smokes, is not for him to smoke. So what about, say, 'I promise'? If the case is analogous, then to say 'I promise', however fully felicitously, while it is to say that I promise, will not be to promise. But surely it is agreed on all hands that that is just what it is.

But this argument fails, I think. It relies on the general principle that to say that one does something is not, and cannot be, to do it—from which, of course, it would follow that promising cannot be saying (however felicitously) *that* one promises, or vice versa. But is this principle true? Very obviously it is true in those many cases, such as that of smoking, where *what* one says that one does, and the question whether or not one does it, is wholly independent of, detachable from, one's saying that, or indeed saying anything at all; but of course, in the case of explicit performatives, we are dealing precisely with things that people do *in* saying things, their doing of which (or not) is therefore *not* independent of what they say. And may it not be precisely here that the principle of the above argument fails, and indeed should be expected to fail? For if to promise, unlike to smoke, is essentially to *say* something, why it should it *not* be to say *that* one promises? Consider a different but obviously kindred case. The notice reads 'Customers are warned not to leave valuables in the cloak-room'. By that notice, customers are warned. But what does the notice *say*? Surely, *it says that they are.* I can see no fissure here between it being said that they are, and their actually being so. Of course, if the notice had read (surprisingly) 'Customers are badly treated here', it would have remained an open question whether or not they were; but that is because the question whether or not they are badly treated, unlike the question whether or not they are warned, is quite independent of what the notice says. Can we not say, in the warning case, that what the notice says—namely, *that* customers are warned—is in effect *made true* by the fact that the notice says it, and hence that saying that customers are warned *is* warning the customers? That the text of the notice sets out, so to speak, to make itself true, and *can* make itself true, is shown, I think, by the fact, noted of course by Austin, that in such a case one can stick in the word 'hereby'; the notice says that customers are warned, not by something or someone *else* who might actually fall down on the job, but hereby, by itself, by this notice, by the very one whose text *says* that customers are warned. 'Hereby' is an indication that the utterance *itself* is doing the job that it says is done.

One might object, more trivially, that while one may indeed, in saying 'I promise', say that one promises, that case is precisely the one in which one does not promise. 'What do you do when your wife complains of your habitual indolence?'—'I promise to work harder.' This, however, is just what we may call the other use of the present tense; and from the fact that if, in saying 'I promise', I mean that I habitually promise, I do not there and then promise, it cannot follow that I do not there and then promise when, in saying 'I promise', I mean that I there and then do. Once again, 'hereby' might come in here as a disambiguating device. If, in saying 'I promise' I think that it might be supposed that I am therein alluding to what I do on some *other* occasions, I could put 'hereby' into my utterance, and thus make it clear that the promising I say that I do is done in this utterance itself, in what I here and now say.

But, an objector might continue, when speaking of what we here and now do, surely we use in English the *continuous* present; when I play cricket, I state what I then do, if I have occasion to do so, in the form 'I am playing cricket'. So if, say in promising, my utterance were to be statementally about what I there and then do, should it not be, as it is not and cannot be, in the form 'I am promising'? But there is not much in this. Explicit performatives, as a matter of fact, occasionally *are* in the continuous present—'I'm warning you' is every bit as common as 'I warn you'. But it is actually not hard to see why, usually, they are not. The continuous present, after all, is most at home with doings one is engaged in which extend, so to speak, beyond the temporal boundaries of one's saying, if one happens to do so, that one is doing them; but with explicit performatives, one's doing the thing coincides with, does *not* temporally over-spread, one's saying that one does it. And in such a case—the case of, so to speak, temporal concurrence of word and deed—in other instances too, it is the non-continuous present tense that one naturally resorts to. Severing the jugular vein of the patient in the operating theatre, I say concurrently and explanatorily to the assembled students 'I sever the jugular vein . . .' Thus, if I am to say *that* I here and now promise, that I should say 'I promise' is exactly what one would expect.

But another snag now awaits us. It was first objected that to say *that* one does something cannot be to do it; I replied that I did not see why that should be so, in the case in which what one does, and says that one does, is itself a piece of *saying*. But, it may then be objected, if that is so, saying for instance, 'I promise' could not be, even if it were saying that one promises, saying so *truly or falsely*. For if I promise *in* saying that I do, what I say would substantiate itself and *could* not be false. (We said just above that the notice 'makes itself true'.) But can that be said to be even true, which could not be said falsely? Now one might, in principle, bluntly counter this move by saying: why not? If my saying that *p* were a fully sufficient condition of its being the case that *p*, then indeed I could not falsely say that *p*; but *that p* could perfectly well be either true or false—true, of course, *ex hypothesi*, if it happens to be said that *p* by me, but perhaps false otherwise (cf. 'I exist', 'I am alive', perhaps 'I am awake'). But in fact we do not need, I believe, that line of defence here; for one can well hold, I think, that one *can* say falsely that one promises (and likewise *mutatis mutandis* for other explicit performatives). For promising is, as we earlier platitudinously remarked, not *just* saying that one does so, just producing that dictum. For it to be the case that one promises, there must (very roughly) be some envisaged commitment, asked for by, or offered to, some second party, which in one's utterance one formally undertakes. If I say here and now 'I promise', out of the blue, I have not—other necessary circumstances being absent in this case—therein promised; so that in such a case, maybe, I say that I promise, but falsely—I do not. (Of course I don't make a false promise—that's a different matter.) This is only to say, I think, that, on this present view as on any other, we must take due account of Austinian infelicities. On any view, I do not promise in saying 'I promise' if the circumstances in which I speak are wrong for the purpose; so that, on my view, it seems it can quite well be held that, in unhappy circumstances, one may say that one promises falsely, when actually one does not. And if it were further objected, as it might well be, that in saying 'I promise', just out of the blue, one cannot be supposed really even to have said that one promised, then I could reply *either* that there are less grossly infelicitous cases in which, though I do seriously say that I promise, it is still not true that I do—*or* that, if it is to be held that one really *says that* one promises when and only when one's utterance is fully felicitous and therefore one promises, I must adopt the blunt fall-back position mentioned above—of maintaining, that is, that there is nothing in principle vicious in the idea of a proposition which, while it can be true or false, can't be falsely asserted, or rather, can't be falsely asserted by a particular person. I do not like that, however, in this present case; it seems to me better to say that, since just saying 'I promise' is not, on any view, the sole and sufficient element in promising, it is possible to say that one promises when one does not, just as—or anyway, somewhat as —it is possible to say that one smokes when one does not. (I repeat that this is not, obviously, the case of a false promise, in which case one does promise, not intending to perform.) In all this, of course, I must not be taken as denying that explicit performative utterances are any sort of special case at all. Obviously, in a way, they are—for they have the peculiarity that, since in these cases what the speaker says that he does is something that is done in speaking, and indeed is in fact done by him (if all goes well) in saying the very thing that he says, the truth-value of what he says is involved (let us say vaguely) in a decidedly unusual way with the fact that he says it. But one can quite well concede, as clearly one must, that explicit performative utterances are a rather peculiar lot in *this* way, without holding that they are peculiar in not having truth-values at all, or in being anomalous, masquerading exceptions to the comfortable principle that one who says something of the form 'I *X*' therein says that he *X*-es.

I want now to turn from thinking up arguments *against* the idea that explicit performatives are not 'masqueraders', and instead to draw attention to one of its significant implications. It would follow, I think, terminologically most inconveniently, that explicit performative utterances are—or at any rate are for the most part—not performative utterances at all, in the original, Mark I sense of that appellation. This is easily seen. It will be recalled that the class of Mark I performative utterances consisted of those which, in virtue of some not simply linguistic convention, counted as, when happily issued, *doing* this or that —as saying, in playing bridge, 'Three no trumps' constitutes *bidding*. But now, if the suggestion I have been putting forward is correct, most (anyway) explicit performatives are not like this at all. For it is surely the position, if I am right, that what makes it the case that, in saying (happily) 'I promise' or 'I advise you to . . .', I promise or advise is, not a convention in virtue of which to speak so counts as or constitutes promising or advising, but simply the standard, normal *meaning* of the words that I utter. I have already suggested that, if I warn you in saying 'The train leaves at three', it is not a convention, but certain facts about the situation, which make it the case that in so speaking I warn you; what I now want to say is that if I warn you *explicitly*, by saying, for instance, 'I warn you that the train leaves at three', it is again no special convention that makes it the case that in so speaking I warn you, but in this case, straightforwardly, the standard meaning of what I say. You will not grasp what I do in saying 'Three no trumps' if, though you understand English, you are unfamiliar with the rules, or with the relevant rule, of bridge; but I suggest that, in order to grasp what I do in saying 'I warn you that . . .', you need no equipment beyond the understanding of English. If that is so, then explicit performatives, for the most part anyway, are not by *convention* operative utterances, to issue which conventionally counts as doing this or that; there are no special conventions; they are indeed utterances in issuing which (happily) this or that is done, but *what* is done is done simply in virtue of what they mean. If that is so, then they are for the most part not Mark I performatives at all. The qualifications are to allow for the fact that they sometimes might be. Where we have, in some game, for instance, some convention-constituted performance *X*-ing, then indeed it might be, though of course it need not be, *by convention* an essential constituent in *X*-ing that the appropriate person is formally to say 'I *X*'. In cricket, for instance, to declare an innings closed, it might have been required by rule that the captain of the batting side should shout *'Basta!'*, or wave his arms at the umpires in some particular manner; but equally it might have been required (though I do not believe it is) that he should formally say 'I declare the innings closed.' Well, *if* the latter had been the case, then the explicit performative 'I declare the innings closed' would not merely have meant that he declared the innings closed, but would also have been *by convention* 'operative' in his actually doing so. The classes, then, of Mark I performatives and of explicit performatives, though they are not the same, could have, quite contingently of course, some members in common.

I can sum up what I have been arguing for in this paper, putting things in a rather different order, as follows:

(1) There is, I suppose, if one chooses to say so, a tolerable sense in which all utterance is, or normally is, performative; whenever anyone speaks there are things—many things of many sorts—that he could be said therein to do; so that we have a general topic, as yet unexhausted nor even very well defined, that we could call the topic of 'speech acts'. We note here that it is not necessarily, though it may be sometimes, in virtue of a *convention* (other than those conventions, if they are such, which give sentences their senses) that to issue a certain utterance is to perform a certain speech act; not all speech acts are 'conventional', though doubtless some are. It will depend mostly, of course, on what species of speech act one is talking about.

(2) The fact that, if we choose to say so, all utterance is in that sense performative does not imply that there is not, and never was, a legitimate *sub-class* of utterances called 'performative', to issue which is in a *special* way to do something; and there seem in fact to be at least two such special sub-classes, very different from each other though having some members in common.

(*a*) First, there is that sub-class of utterances the issuing of which *by convention* (over and above what, if anything, the words uttered conventionally mean) is 'operative' in the doing of this or that; put otherwise, there is a class of conventional acts which can be, or normally are, or even necessarily are, done *by* the utterance of certain conventionally prescribed words; in such cases, the utterance is 'operative' in a *special* way, and can be said in a *special* sense to be a performative utterance. There is, however, no special verbal form that such utterances have to take; there is no reason why they should not sometimes take the form of saying something which is true or false; the word *for* what is done in issuing them *may*, by convention, be required to figure in the utterance, possibly in the first person present indicative active, but there is no particular reason why that should be so, and very often it is not so. Finally, one who does something by issuing an utterance of this sort does not necessarily, or even usually, say *in* his utterance that he does the thing in question.

(*b*) Then there is another sub-class of utterances, identifiable by the purely formal special feature that, being in the first person present indicative active (I omit, merely for brevity, the familiar passive form), they have as main verb the *word for* what (one thing which) a speaker would be said to do in issuing them. This sub-class is importantly distinct from the former one in two major respects—first, that its members, unlike those of the former one, are all by definition of a certain verbal form; and second, that it is not, as in the former case it was, necessarily, or even often, *by convention* that to issue the utterance is to do the thing. At any rate in my submission, we can quite well hold here that the speaker, in his utterance, says *that* he does the thing in question—so that, first, such utterances can be construed as perfectly regular, non-anomalous, unexceptional, non-masquerading uses of the first person present indicative active, and second, *what* the speaker does is usually a function, not of any special convention, but simply of the standard meaning of what he says. There may, however, occur the special case in which saying that one does something does happen to be, by convention, an essential 'operative' element in actually doing it; and in that case, members of this second sub-class will also be members of the former one.

Well, perhaps that all seems very obvious, and indeed I hope it does. Historically, what has I think tended to obscure the issue is (1) that Austin, from the beginning, introduced *simultaneously* the above two sub-classes—conventionally 'operative' utterances, and explicit performative utterances—without explicitly saying, and without perhaps always or wholly clearly seeing, that he had got in the hand two birds of very different feather, not one bird; and (2) that, when he moved on from *special* ways of being performative to consider those many ways in which all utterance could, if one likes, be called performative, he certainly sometimes gave, and it is hard not to think that he also sometimes got, the mistaken impression that the special ways of being performative had turned out to be somehow illusory, that in some way or other the 'original' distinction had, as he sometimes said himself and as others have said too, 'broken down'. Once we have firmly made what I hope are some decently clear and defensible distinctions here, we might perhaps be further assisted by some new terminology; perhaps the *word* 'performative' really has rather broken down, under the strain of being given too many different jobs to do, and might usefully in future be relieved of some of its duties. But I have no particular terminological innovations to suggest.

VI

Ifs and Cans[1]

D. F. PEARS

AUSTIN's lecture on this topic contributes little to the problem of freedom of the will, and so in my discussion of his ideas I shall stop short of the difficult part of that problem. His most important positive suggestion is that hypotheticals should be divided into two classes, conditionals and pseudo-conditionals. He claims that neglect of this distinction has been the cause of mistakes in certain forms of the dispositional analysis of the statement that an agent could have acted otherwise, and he then goes on to criticize all forms of that analysis using arguments which do not depend on the difference between the two kinds of hypothetical.

This discussion will be in two parts. In the first I shall take up Austin's distinction between conditionals and pseudos and criticize it and develop it at length, because it seems to me to be the most important thing in his lecture. Since I shall not have space for comment on fortuitous errors made by defenders of the dispositional analysis of the claim that an agent could have acted otherwise, I shall concentrate on the essential features of that analysis. My investigation of the differences between the two kinds of hypothetical will lead to further distinctions which can be used in defence of the general idea expressed in dispositional analyses of ascriptions of powers, abilities, and capacities. So in Part I of this discussion I shall develop Austin's main idea in a direction that is approximately the opposite of his line of argument.

In Part II I shall examine some general attacks on all forms of the dispositional analysis of such ascriptions. Most of these

[1] This article is here reprinted from volume 1, nos. 2 and 3 of the *Canadian Journal of Philosophy*, by permission of the Canadian Association for Publishing in Philosophy.

general criticisms are developed in Austin's lecture. But I shall also examine a criticism which has been devised more recently by K. Lehrer.[2] My disagreement with Austin in this field will be more direct than it is in Part I. But, though I shall try to show that his arguments do not support his complete rejection of the dispositional analysis, I think that one of them does lead to an equally important, if not quite so ambitious, conclusion.

I

Austin distinguishes conditionals from pseudos in the following way: a hypothetical is a conditional if and only if it entails its contrapositive—otherwise it is a pseudo.[3] For example, the hypothetical 'I can pay you tomorrow if I choose' is a pseudo by this contrapositive test. This is a good way of drawing the distinction, because it is natural to call a hypothetical a conditional when and only when the truth of the antecedent is put forward as a sufficient condition of the truth of the consequent, and when and only when this is its point the hypothetical passes the contrapositive test for conditionality.

There is, of course, nothing wrong with a pseudo. The only reason for giving it this faintly pejorative name is that the conditional use of 'if' is its central and most frequent use. So those who argue, as I shall argue in this paper, that some pseudos contain a conditional 'if' in a special subordinate position, need not be suffering from the prejudice that all occurrences of 'if' have to be accounted for in some such way. The justification of this kind of account is its explanatory power, if it fits. It is based on the central and most frequent use of 'if', and so, when it can be extended to outlying cases, it will explain them very well.

After drawing this clear distinction, Austin complicates it by bringing in a second test of conditionality. According to the second test a hypothetical is a conditional if and only if it does not entail its detached consequent.[4] The hypothetical 'I can pay you tomorrow if I choose' also fails this second test for conditionality, and so comes out again as a pseudo. This test might be

[2] 'An Empirical Disproof of Determinism' in *Freedom and Determinism*, ed. K. Lehrer (1966).
[3] *Philosophical Papers* (Oxford, 1961), p. 157. All references to Austin's British Academy lecture 'Ifs and Cans' (1956) will be to this reprint in *Philosophical Papers* (first edition).   [4] Ibid., p. 157.

called the non-detachment test. Naturally, the use of both tests should be restricted to cases in which neither the antecedent nor the consequent is analytic or self-contradictory.

There are difficulties about the use of these two tests for conditionality. First, it might be argued that they give divergent results for the hypothetical 'He can do it if he chooses.' This hypothetical is in fact used to ascribe ability and opportunity to the agent, but it might conceivably be made to include the implication that he can choose to do it—or, to put this in more natural English, that he can bring himself to do it. So someone might argue that it does not entail its detached consequent (in spite of not entailing its contrapositive), on the ground that it might be true that the agent had the ability and opportunity, but not true that he could bring himself to do it.[5] But against this argument we could defend Austin's simultaneous use of both his tests for conditionality by pointing out that he was not expanding the verb 'can' so as to include the implication that the agent could bring himself to do it. When 'He can do it' only ascribes ordinary ability and opportunity to the agent, it really is entailed by the original hypothetical. So Austin could have maintained that his two tests for conditionality do not diverge in this case, provided that the meaning of 'He can do it' is not expanded. This defence of his position amounts to inter-preting the detached consequent in the following way: 'He can do it, whether or not, perhaps *per impossibile*, he chooses to do it.'

However, this is not a complete defence of his position, because the two tests for conditionality really would produce divergent results if we did pack the extra implication into the expanding suitcase 'can'. But we can complete the defence by making two further points. First, if the 'can' in the detached consequent included the extra implication, then so too would the 'can' in the original hypothetical. But, secondly, though the 'can' in the original hypothetical might conceivably be *given* this meaning, it certainly does not already have it. For, as I shall show later, 'He can if he chooses' is used to convey the informa-tion that the agent's choosing would close the gap between the

---

[5] R. Chisholm emphasizes this possibility in a different context in his review of *Philosophical Papers*, *Mind* (1964), part of which is reprinted in *Free Will and Determinism*, ed. B. Berofsky (1966).

existing situation and his performance. It goes as far as, and no farther than, an ordinary ascription of ability and opportunity. Naturally, the more difficult part of the problem of freedom of the will is not touched by these defences of Austin's thesis that 'He can do it if he chooses' entails 'He can do it'.

There is another kind of case in which it is difficult to apply Austin's two tests, not because they give divergent results, but because neither of them seems to be applicable. An example of this kind would be the hypothetical 'This van can do 70 m.p.h. if it is unloaded'.[6] If this hypothetical is taken as a conditional ascription of the unconditional power to do 70 m.p.h., there is no difficulty. For, on that interpretation it clearly passes both the contrapositive test and the non-detachment test for conditionality. The difficulty arises if we take it as an unconditional ascription of the conditional power to do, if it is unloaded, 70 m.p.h. For, on this interpretation, the questions whether it entails its contrapositive or its detached consequent do not seem to arise.[7] This is because, when the hypothetical is construed in this way, the antecedent is used in the specification of the ascribed power, and so is no longer available to fill the grammatical role of governing the main verb which ascribes it. It is therefore impossible to write down the contrapositive of the ascription, and impossible to regard its affirmation as the affirmation of a detached consequent. So here is an example of a pseudo for which Austin's tests for conditionality cannot be set up. Yet it seems quite legitimate to interpret the hypothetical as a pseudo, unconditionally ascribing a conditional power. In fact I shall try to show later that, when the antecedent in a hypothetical ascribing a power or ability introduces a factor which contributes to specifying that power or ability, we nearly always have an option between the two interpretations, conditional and pseudo, and that we sometimes have a good reason for choosing the pseudo interpretation. In such a case the explanation of the lack of a contrapositive is simple: we have chosen to put the antecedent of the original hypothetical to another use. It is not that we are forced to give it another use,

---

[6] M. R. Ayers discusses examples of this kind in *The Refutation of Determinism* (1968), ch. 5. Though my treatment of them differs from his, I agree with his idea that Austin's concept of a pseudo ought somehow to be applicable to this kind of example too.

[7] This point was made by Richard Malpas in discussion.

because the hypothetical does not pass the contrapositive test: rather, we choose to give it another use, and so there is no contrapositive test.

This, of course, is not a case in which Austin's two tests give divergent results, but one in which it is difficult to apply his his tests at all. If, gratuitously, we placed the antecedent 'If it is unloaded . . .' in front of the ascription of the conditional power 'It can do, if it is unloaded, 70', the two tests could be applied, and would give the same result. For this new hypothetical would not entail its contrapositive (we would not deduce that, if the van lacks the conditional power, it is loaded), and it would entail its detached consequent (we would deduce that it possesses the conditional power, whether or not it is unloaded: for unloading it does not give it the power to do, if unloaded, 70). But in fact it is gratuitous to write in the antecedent a second time, and it is better to say that this kind of pseudo does not fail Austin's tests for conditionality, but, rather, fails to qualify to take them. The explanation of this radical failure is simply our choice of interpretation.

There is, however, another way of looking at the pseudo interpretation of this hypothetical. Without writing in the antecedent a second time, we could say that someone who takes the hypothetical as a pseudo is simply interpreting it as not entailing its contrapositive. Having taken that decision, he then asks himself what he should do about the antecedent, and his solution to this problem is to construe it as qualifying the complementary verb 'do 70'. Now this explanation has a point. The understanding of the hypothetical does involve two stages, the realization that the antecedent does not govern the main verb, and the realization that it does govern the subordinate verb, and this explanation takes these two steps separately in this order, whereas the other explanation takes them in one stride. But though there is a point in the stepwise explanation, which would allow us to write down the contrapositive of the original hypothetical, it is unclear and confusing. For if we split the application of the tests into these two stages, we get an incoherent account of the tester's process of thought. For how can he deny that the hypothetical entails its contrapositive unless he has already attached the antecedent to the subordinate verb? And, if he has attached it to the subordinate verb, how can he write down the contrapositive of the unconditional ascription of the conditional power? So let us adhere to the other explanation, which takes the two stages in one stride, and so achieves a more realistic account of what the tester does in cases like these in which he exercises an option.

The application of Austin's tests to this example suggests the question whether the subordinate phrase 'do, if it is unloaded, 70' passes Austin's two tests, and so comes out as a subordinate conditional. Or do his two tests perhaps give divergent results for this subordinate phrase? But this question may be deferred for the moment. Meanwhile let us look at a case in which the application of his two tests to the main part of a hypothetical clearly produces divergent results.

Consider the following example, in which the hypothetical does not pass the contrapositive test for conditionality, but in which the antecedent does not add a further specification to the task. A chess player says 'I can resign if I choose.' Here there is no option, and we have to say that the hypothetical does not entail its contrapositive. But the antecedent certainly does not add a further specification to the task—resigning. For there are not two ways of resigning, by choice and not by choice, as there are, for some people, two ways of shedding tears.[8] If we take this hypothetical and negate both the antecedent and the consequent, we get: 'I can not resign if I do not choose to'. This hypothetical too seems to fail the contrapositive test, and again we do not seem to have the alternative opinion of construing it as the conditional denial of an unconditional power. However, this is denied by Keith Lehrer, who uses a similar example in his article 'An Empirical Disproof of Determinism?',[9] but construes it as a hypothetical which may be allowed to pass the contrapositive test for conditionality. I disagree with his treatment of such examples, and I shall explain why I disagree later. At present, it is sufficient to point out that, if a chess player said 'I can not resign if I do not choose to', he would certainly mean it as a hypothetical which failed the contrapositive test for conditionality. Admittedly, it would be an odd thing to say, because there is only one way of resigning, by choice—or, to

---

[8] Norman Dahl pointed out that in discussion the importance of this difference between verbs of action in the investigation of the logic of pseudos.

[9] Loc. cit.

put this in a way that connects it with the hypotheticals about the van, the words, 'by choice' do not add a further specification to resigning, but designate something which is already included in the meaning of that verb. It follows that the chess player would have to be making an *a priori* statement about resigning. No doubt, this is odd, but, if he made the remark, he would certainly mean it in this way. But equally certainly it would not fail the non-detachment test for conditionality. For from the fact that he cannot resign without choosing to, it evidently does not follow that he cannot resign. So here is a case which exhibits a clear divergence between Austin's two tests.

This example introduces some very complex considerations, which I shall try to unravel later. We may wonder how Austin's two tests can possibly give divergent results for hypotheticals of any kind. But I want to defer the explanation of this phenomenon. It is enough for my present purpose that the phenomenon exists, and that Austin's two tests really do give divergent results with this kind of hypothetical. This ought to make us very cautious about the simultaneous use of the two tests, and from now on I shall use only the contrapositive test. A hypothetical is a pseudo if and only if it fails the contrapositive test for conditionality. Some pseudos entail their detached consequents, while others do not—a difference which needs to be explained.

The antecedent in a pseudo does not govern the main verb. So perhaps in some cases it governs the subordinate verb.[10] For example, in the pseudo 'I can pay you tomorrow if I choose', since the antecedent does not govern the main verb 'can', perhaps it governs the subordinate verb 'pay'. This is a grammatical possibility. But it is closely linked with the semantic possibility that the antecedent in a pseudo combines with the subordinate verb to form a subordinate conditional—i.e. a conditional which somehow falls within the scope of the main verb. This suggestion is not an unfamiliar one. It is natural to treat 'It is possible that . . .' as an operator followed by brackets which sometimes contain a molecular proposition, and the suggestion that is here being put forward amounts to extending

---

[10] As far as I know, this suggestion about pseudos in which 'can' is the main verb was first made by Don Locke in 'Ifs and Cans Revisited', *Philosophy* (1962), Cf. M. R. Ayers, op. cit., p. 101.

this treatment to ascriptions of power or ability. The difficulty is to see exactly how such ascriptions would then be understood.

A clear case of a hypothetical with this structure would be the expression of a conditional intention—e.g. 'I intend to pay him if he asks me', which evidently means that I intend to, if he asks me, pay him. But is 'I can' amenable to this treatment? The fact that 'It is possible that . . .' may be treated as an operator might encourage us to treat 'I can' as an operator too. But it is notorious that the general claim 'I can do it' does not mean the same thing as 'It is possible that I should do it'. So, if the suggestion is going to work, some account must be given of the special semantics of conditionals subordinated to the main verb 'can' in pseudos ascribing powers or abilities.

It seems to me to be easier to give such an account for hypotheticals like 'This van can do 70 if it is unloaded' than it is for hypotheticals like 'I can pay you tomorrow if I choose'. So I shall begin with hypotheticals of the first of these two types.

'This van can do 70 if it is unloaded.' I pointed out earlier that we have an option between the two interpretations of this hypothetical: we can take it either as a conditional or as a pseudo. This option is explicable. For the hypothetical gives a general specification of what the van can do, and the antecedent contributes something important to the specification. Consequently we may read it in either of two ways: either as a conditional saying that lack of a load would give the van the unconditional power to do 70, or as a pseudo saying that it unconditionally has the power to do 70 without a load. Let me call lack of a load a 'performance-specifying factor' or '*S*-factor' for short. Then an *S*-factor, introduced in the antecedent of a hypothetical ascribing a power or ability to a thing or person, may be regarded in either of two ways: either as something that pushes the power up to the level of a completely specified task—in this example, doing 70—or as something that pushes the task down within reach of the power—i.e. pushes it down because the speaker adds it as a further specification which makes it easier—in this example, the task is then finally specified as doing 70 unloaded.

There are three features of this explanation which ought to be emphasized. First, the antecedent is always taken as offering a sufficient condition—of the power going up, on the conditional interpretation, and of the task coming down, on the pseudo interpretation. The word 'if' sometimes conversationally impli-cates[11] 'and only if'. But that is a complication which it would take too long to investigate.

Secondly, not all *S*-factors make the task easier. Lack of a load happens to be a facilitating *S*-factor. But presence of a load is an impeding *S*-factor. So the hypothetical 'This van can do 70 if it is loaded' needs a more elaborate explanation. The word 'if' in this case means 'even if', and so, when the hypothetical is taken as a pseudo, its point is that the load does not push the task up beyond the reach of the van's power—i.e. that it does not push it up out of reach although the speaker adds the fact that it is loaded as a further specification which makes it more difficult. But this too is a complication which lies off my route.

Thirdly, when the word 'if' does not mean 'even if', the *S*-factor need not be exactly facilitating. Facilitation is a matter of degree, and is often associated with a scale. But an *S*-factor might involve a difference of kind, which pushed the task over a sharp edge into the domain of feasibility.

My aim in this section is to show that, when the hypothetical 'This van can do 70 if it is unloaded' is taken as a pseudo, it contains a subordinate conditional. That is, I hope to show that, on this interpretation, the antecedent governs the subordinate verb 'do 70', and that this grammatical partnership expresses an ordinary conditional connection between the *S*-factor mentioned in the antecedent and the action of the subordinate verb. If this is right, the only unusual feature of the example will be that the conditional is a subordinate one, falling within the scope of the main verb 'can'. Since I am using the contrapositive test for conditionality, it follows that, in order to establish this point, I shall have to demonstrate that the original sentence entails another which is derived from it by contraposing the subordi-nate phrase 'do if it is unloaded 70'. As I remarked at the begin-ning, we do not need to be prejudiced in favour of this theory. Its merit is its explanatory power, if it fits.

But before I develop this theory, more needs to be said about the option between the conditional and pseudo interpretations

[11] See Paul Grice, 'The Causal Theory of Perception', *Proceedings of the Aristotelian Society*, supp. vol. xxxv (1961), pp. 126–32 for an early sketch of his theory.

of the hypothetical 'This van can do 70 if it is unloaded'. The option is puzzling, because it is not clear exactly what is at stake. It is evident that the truth-conditions of the hypothetical will be the same, whichever way it is taken. So the difference between the two interpretations can only be a difference between two ways of looking at the same facts—either as the conditional possession of an unconditional power, or as the unconditional possession of a conditional power.

But on what does the option depend? If I am right, it is open to us when and only when the factor introduced in the antecedent is an *S*-factor, like lack of a load. Choosing, on the other hand, is usually not an *S*-factor. In fact, choosing cannot be an *S*-factor when it is choosing to perform an action which is specified in a way that implies that it is a full human action, like paying a debt or resigning at chess. So choosing is not an *S*-factor in the hypothetical 'I can resign if I choose'. Consequently we do not have the option of treating this hypothetical as a conditional. It simply cannot mean that my choosing would push my ability up to the level of the specified task,[12] and so we are forced to take it as a pseudo. Moreover, when it is taken as a pseudo, it will not mean that my choosing, added as a further specificatory factor, would push the task down within reach of my ability. When choosing is not an *S*-factor, as it is not in these cases, we are forced not only to adopt the pseudo interpretation, but also to understand the pseudo in a different way, which I shall try to explain later.

Choosing, if it is choosing to perform an action specified in a way that implies that it is a full human action, is not the only example of a factor that is not an *S*-factor, when it is introduced in the antecedent of a hypothetical which has 'can' as the main verb of its consequent. Another example would be wanting, as it occurs in 'I can pay you tomorrow if I want to'. The verbs 'can' and 'be able' need not occur in such sentences: for instance, neither of these two verbs occurs in the sentence 'He was clever enough to have been a doctor if he had wanted to be one', and yet it has the same structure. In these last two examples, it is, of course, conceivable that wanting is being put forward as an *S*-factor which would increase, or would have

[12] See Part II for the discussion of Keith Lehrer's view that it might have this meaning.

increased, the agent's ability. But it is much more likely that it is not being put forward as an *S*-factor, and so that the two hypotheticals are meant as pseudos to be understood in a way that will be explained later. I hope to show eventually that the contrast between *S*-factors and non-*S*-factors is closely connected both with the distinction between conditionals and pseudos and with certain problems in the dispositional analysis of ascriptions of power and ability.

It is evident that the application of the term '*S*-factor' is relative to the kind of verb which designates the performance. It is also relative to the nature of the subject to which the power or ability is ascribed. Suppose, for example, that my car is a Morris Minor and I say 'It could do 150 if it were an E-type Jaguar'. Then, although being an E-type Jaguar makes that performance feasible, it cannot be classified as an *S*-factor. For the power to do 150 if it is an E-type Jaguar is a power whose specification involves a change of identity in the subject to which it is, as a matter of fact, being ascribed. If the antecedent were fulfilled, we would not say that my car had been changed into an E-type Jaguar; we would say, rather, that I had exchanged my car for an E-type Jaguar. So here we have an example of a factor which is similar to an *S*-factor—unlike choosing, which in the cases specified above is quite dissimilar—but which is just beyond the limit of that classification.

But, to return to the option between the two interpretations of a single hypothetical, what is at stake? In cases which leave the option open to us, what inclines us to one interpretation rather than to the other? I do not want to answer this question in detail, because it lies off my route. It is evident that in general the choice is governed by two considerations, the kind of subject to which the power or ability is being ascribed and the context of the ascription. Suppose, for example, that a salesman says 'This car can do 120 if it is filled with high-octane petrol'. This general statement, in this context, would naturally be taken as an unconditional ascription of a conditional power. On the other hand, if he said 'This car can do 120 if its compression ratio is increased', this would naturally be taken in the other way, because the conversion of an engine is a big alteration to a car. However, in certain contexts, even this statement could be taken as an unconditional ascription of a conditional power—

e.g. in a conversation between two mechanics. As we have seen, the absolute limit to the possibility of this interpretation has been passed when the fulfilment of the antecedent would change the identity of the subject. Probably we ought to move this limit one step further inwards, and insist that the fulfilment of the antecedent should leave some basic determinant properties of the subject unchanged: e.g. in the conversation between the two mechanics the point is that the other properties of the car are such that it actually is capable of doing, if its compression ratio is changed, 120.[13]

Much more could be said about the option. But I must now develop the thesis that, when such hypotheticals are taken as pseudos, the antecedent governs the subordinate verb both grammatically and semantically, and that this partnership expresses a subordinate conditional.

I am not sure how important for my purpose it is to establish that the antecedent governs the subordinate verb grammatically, or how much can be done to establish this point without the support of a general grammatical theory. My thesis rests mainly on the plausibility of the semantic analysis which I am going to put forward. But there seems to be some fairly strong evidence to be collected from the grammar of these hypotheticals.

The first point to notice about their grammar is that the verbs 'can' and 'be able' belong to the class of auxiliary verbs which show some independence in their behaviour. For they are not used merely in order to form tenses and moods of other verbs. In the sentence 'He could have taken that trick if he had been leading',[14] the verb 'could' maintains a degree of independence,

---

[13] M. R. Ayers argues that our choice between the two interpretations follows the line dividing the subject's intrinsic properties from its extrinsic properties (op. cit., ch. 5). But context also seems to exert an influence, and even, in some cases, to help us to answer the question, which properties of the subject should be treated as basic.

[14] This sentence means that he had the capacity, and that if he had also had the opportunity nothing would have prevented him from taking the trick. But it could convey this message in either of two ways. Nowell-Smith suggests one of them in 'Ifs and Cans' (*Theoria*, 1960, reprinted in Berofsky, op. cit.: see pp. 325–6): he takes the main verb to *mean* 'nothing would have prevented him', and then the hypothetical is inevitably interpreted as a conditional. However, if it is not contradictory to treat 'nothing prevented him' (i.e. 'all-in could') as an operator with a subordinate conditional in its scope—and I suppose that it is not contradictory—it would be possible to interpret the main verb as 'nothing prevented him', and the rest of the sentence as a subordinate conditional, 'from, if he had been leading, taking the

and does not lose its natural grammatical rights in slavery to the complementary verb 'take'. Of course, it must have a complementary verb, and it is for this reason that it is classified as an auxiliary, but the relationship between it and its complement is on more equal terms than the relationship between the verbs 'will/would' and 'shall/should' and their complements. These verbs are usually slavish auxiliaries to their complements. For example, in the sentence 'He would have taken that trick if he had been leading', the verb 'would' is totally used up in the task of forming a tense and mood of the complementary verb 'take'.

Although this is the usual lot of the verbs 'will/would', and 'shall/should', it is an interesting fact that they sometimes cast off their shackles and achieve the same degree of independence as the verbs 'can' and 'be able'. This certainly happens in emphatic statements of intention, like 'I will not pay that tax'. But even in this example we should not discount the possibility that an ordinary future-tense statement is somehow implied. Austin argues that the verb 'would' achieves the higher degree of independence in the sentence 'X would have hanged him, but Y was against it'.[15] His idea is that the first part means that X actually wished to have hanged him. This may be an exaggeration of the force of the verb 'would' in this sentence, but there is no doubt that this element is an essential part of at least some statements of intention.[16]

It is an important fact that the verb 'can' always enjoys this degree of independence. For it makes it possible in certain cases for us to vary the moods of the main verb 'can' and of its complementary verb, independently of one another, in order to convey a double message in an economical way. This can be illustrated by the previous example. The speaker wanted to convey two pieces of information in one hypothetical—that the player had the capacity to take the trick, and that he did not take it because he lacked the opportunity. The first piece of

trick'. The sentence would then be a pseudo. (This treatment depends, of course, on the validity of the theory of subordinate conditionals.) Austin interprets the sentence as a pseudo, but in a more natural way than this, because he takes the main verb to mean 'he had the capacity' (op. cit., pp. 177–8). All these interpretations are viable, but Austin's needs some refinement, because he needs to explain the implication of the complementary phrase 'have taken'.

[15] Austin, op. cit., p. 168, note 2.

[16] See G. Anscombe, *Intention* (1957), *passim*, and A. Kenny, *Action, Emotion and Will* (1961), ch. 11.

information is conveyed by the verb 'could', interpreted, as Austin interprets it, as a past indicative unconditionally ascribing a conditional capacity to the player (I am here following the pseudo interpretation of the hypothetical, although, as I said, it is not obligatory). The second piece of information is conveyed by the time-shifted perfect infinitive 'have taken' and the time-shifted quasi-subjunctive 'had been leading'.

If this account of the passing of the two pieces of information is going to work, it needs to be supplemented with an explanation of the function of the time-shift towards the past. The explanation is that in English it is possible to shift the tense of a verb one step backwards in time as a substitute for the true subjunctive mood. For example, we say 'If Hannibal had marched on Rome . . .' rather than 'If Hannibal marched on Rome . . .', and this is a way of implying that he did not march. The strength of this implication must not be exaggerated: sometimes we use the backward time-shift, like the true subjunctive mood, to express a lesser degree of remoteness from actuality—e.g. the case is problematical.[17] But, whatever the exact strength of the implication, a time-shifted quasi-subjunctive, when it is subordinated to a verb like 'can', automatically goes into the perfect infinitive. Thus we arrive at 'He could have taken that trick if he had been leading', and 'He was clever enough to have been a doctor, if he had wanted to be one'. In these cases the ability and cleverness are said to have been actual, but the implication, such as it is, of the perfect infinitives is that the performances were not actual. So the fact that the verb 'can' is an auxiliary with this degree of independence is a semantically important fact. It enables us in certain cases to vary the moods of the main verb and of its complement independently of one another, in order to convey a double message in an economical way. But it must be observed that 'could have' is not always analysable in this way. 'Could have' must mean 'would have been able to', when these hypotheticals are interpreted as conditionals, and sometimes they must be interpreted as conditionals (sometimes they cannot be, and sometimes there is an option).

The possibility of analysing the grammatical structure of these pseudos in this way provides some support for my thesis that they contain subordinate conditionals. But I am not sure how

17 See R. Chisholm, op. cit., p. 343.

much support it provides. In any case, it is far more important for me to establish that a complementary verb-phrase like 'to, if it is unloaded, do 70' really does pass the contrapositive test for conditionality.

It seems that this phrase does pass the contrapositive test. For the hypothetical 'This van can do 70 if it is unloaded' gives the measure of the van's power, and, when it is taken as a pseudo, it does this by specifying the task in a way that is sufficient to bring it down within its reach. So, on this interpretation it says that the van has a power such that the task, doing 70, if it is 70 without a load, is a task that it can do. Now this entails that the van has a power such that the task, doing 70, if it is a task that it cannot do, is 70 with a load. But in this entailed statement the hypothetical in the specificatory consecutive clause has simply been contraposed. Therefore, in this case the antecedent really does govern the subordinate verb, producing in this way a subordinate conditional. This result may be generalized to all hypotheticals which have 'can' or 'be able' as their main verbs and antecedents introducing S-factors. When a hypothetical of this kind is taken as a pseudo, the antecedent governs the complementary verb in the usual conditional way and this partnership may be bracketed to show that it falls within the scope of the operator 'X has a power such that . . .'. Such pseudos may be called 'integrated pseudos', because the antecedent is integrated into the structure of the sentence.

It is no objection to these paraphrases of integrated pseudos to point out that their main sentences contain the word 'power' and that their specificatory consecutive clauses contain the word 'can'. For the paraphrases are not intended to analyse ascriptions of power or ability. They are only intended to display the logical structure of those ascriptions that are pseudos. So it is no fault that each of them contains an occurrence—in fact, two correlative occurrences—of words in the 'can' family. This would be a fault only if they were intended as analyses.

However, it is necessary to say something about the meaning of the operator 'X has a power such that . . .'. It is, as I mentioned earlier, notorious that it means more than 'It is possible that X . . .'. For at least in cases of human agents and usable objects the ascription of a power, capacity, or ability requires more than that its exercise should be consistent with all known facts and laws. Now it is plausible to suppose that the extra requirement is that there is some identifiable initiating factor (*I*-factor), given which and given opportunity, performance will ensue, or, at least, will ensue in a high enough proportion of cases. If this is right, the ascription will entail that, if this *I*-factor is present, then, given the opportunity, the performance will ensue, or at least that this will happen sufficiently often. Omitting the qualifications, we might say that *P* entails *If Q then R*. This, of course, is the idea behind the attempt to analyse such ascriptions dispositionally. The attempt is not entirely successful, because it runs into difficulties more serious than the complications which have just been mentioned. *Q* itself may be partly dispositional, and it may even entail *If P then R*. Moreover, the meaning of *P* may not be completely exhausted by its entailed hypothetical *If Q then R*. In fact, if *Q* does entail *If P then R*, it looks as if *P* and *Q* will each require an attachment to the world that is independent of its entailed hypothetical. Nevertheless it may still be true that *P* does entail *If Q then R*.

If this is true, then the way to eliminate the word 'can' from the consecutive clause specifying the power of the van would be to insert a second antecedent introducing an appropriate *I*-factor: e.g. 'This van has a power such that the task, doing 70, if the task is doing 70 without a load, and if it is driven with the throttle fully open, is one which it will perform.' This more elaborate consecutive clause is at least part of the analysis of the ascription of the power to the van, because, given the opportunity, and allowing for an imperfect success-rate, it is entailed by it. But it is equally clear that this consecutive clause too passes the contrapositive test for conditionality. For the whole proposition now entails that this van has a power such that, if it does not do 70, then either the task is 70 with a load, or it is not being driven with the throttle fully open. Therefore, even when we change the consecutive clause to bring it closer to an analysis of the ascription of the power, it still passes the contrapositive test, and so the original hypothetical still contains a subordinate conditional.

Let me now pick up a question which I dropped earlier, the question whether Austin's two tests for conditionality sometimes give divergent results. I argued that, when they are applied to the hypothetical 'I cannot resign if I do not choose to', they inevitably give divergent results. Let us now ask whether they give divergent results when they are applied to the subordinate phrase in the hypothetical now under examination, 'do, if it is unloaded, 70 m.p.h.'.

It has just been shown that this subordinate phrase does entail its contrapositive. So the next question is: Does it entail its detached consequent? That is, when the hypothetical is taken as a pseudo, unconditionally ascribing a conditional power, does it entail that the van can do 70? If it does, then the subordinate phrase will fail the non-detachment test for conditionality, in spite of passing the contrapositive test.

In fact, there is a strong case for saying that the original hypothetical, taken as a pseudo, does entail that the van can do 70. However, though the conclusion follows, and so, given the truth of the premiss, must be true, it offers a misleadingly incomplete specification of the van's power. So we would never assert it in a context governed by a higher standard of completeness of specification. But the premiss itself sets a higher standard. Therefore, we would never draw the conclusion unless we heavily emphasized the word '*can*'. It seems, then, that though there is a strong case for saying that, when Austin's two tests are applied to the subordinate phrase in this hypothetical, they give divergent results, there is also something to be said on the other side.

It is, perhaps, worth while to look at the related example 'This van cannot do 70 if it is loaded'. When this hypothetical is taken as a pseudo, unconditionally denying a conditional power, its subordinate phrase passes the contrapositive test for conditionality. For if the van's power is such that the task, doing 70, if the task is 70 with a load, is one which it cannot perform, it follows that it is such that, the task, doing 70, if it is one which it can perform, is 70 without a load. But does the subordinate phrase pass the non-detachment test for conditionality? Unlike the subordinate phrase in the previous example, it passes it convincingly. For from the fact that it cannot do 70 when loaded, it does not follow that it cannot do 70. So the original hypothetical, taken as a pseudo, does not entail that the van cannot do 70, and in this case there is no need to bring in the context. Austin's two tests, applied to this subordinate phrase, give the same result in a straightforward way.

This lack of symmetry between the subordinate phrases in

these last two examples can be explained. The explanation is that there is a disanalogy masked by an analogy. The analogy is that the positive hypothetical entails that there are some further specifications of the task, doing 70, which bring it within reach of the van's power; and, similarly, the negative hypothetical entails that there are some further specifications which push it out of reach of the van's power. So far the two cases are symmetrical, and we might suppose that in both cases the detached consequent of the subordinate phrase is entailed, and that in both cases the only odd thing about discarding the antecedent is the misleading omission of the further specifications of the task. But this would exaggerate the symmetry. For there is also an underlying disanalogy. Although the conclusion 'It can do 70' follows from the premiss that there are circumstances in which it can do 70' the conclusion 'It can not do 70' does not follow from the premiss that there are circumstances in which it cannot do 70. For the statement that it cannot do 70 means that there are no circumstances in which it can do 70. The difference lies in the relationship between the two quantified corollaries of the original hypotheticals and the two conclusions that we draw when we discard the antecedents. In the positive case the conclusion does follow from the quantified corollary of the original hypothetical, but in the negative case it does not. So if we discard the antecedent in the positive hypothetical, and draw the conclusion, the only oddity is that the van's power is incompletely specified, whereas, if we discard the antecedent in the negative hypothetical, the conclusion is a *non sequitur*.

This explanation of the asymmetry between the positive and negative examples relies on the tacit assumption that to drive a van loaded and to drive it unloaded are both normal uses of it. For the range of values of the variable of further specifications of the task must be restricted in this way. In this case the two further specifications do fall within the restricted range, and so all is well.

It appears, then, that Austin's simultaneous use of his two tests for conditionality can be more or less vindicated in these cases, in spite of certain difficulties. But earlier we found one example in which it cannot be vindicated. For when the tests are applied to the hypothetical 'I cannot resign if I do not choose to', they clearly give divergent results—which is a surprising result. What is the explanation of the divergence in this outlying type of case?

First, it must be remembered that this hypothetical does not allow the tester an option between the two interpretations, conditional and pseudo. He writes down its contrapositive, finds that it is not entailed and draws the unavoidable conclusion that the hypothetical is not a conditional. The reason why he cannot avoid this conclusion is that choosing, in relation to resigning, is not an *S*-factor, but rather a logically necessary adjunct of resigning.

Now, to develop a point that was made earlier, the stepwise account of the tester's process of thought is realistic in this case: i.e. first he finds that the hypothetical does not entail its contrapositive, and then he asks himself what he should do with the antecedent. The reason why this account is realistic in this case is that he is forced to interpret the hypothetical as a pseudo, whereas in cases which allow an option between the two interpretations, conditional and pseudo, the stepwise account is not realistic, because he has no reason to interpret the hypothetical as a pseudo unless he has already attached the antecedent to the subordinate verb.

When he asks himself what he should do with the antecedent of the hypothetical 'I cannot resign if I do not choose to', his solution may be to attach it to the subordinate verb, taking the pseudo as integrated. But, if he does take this line, he cannot interpret this pseudo exactly like the pseudo 'This van cannot do, if it is loaded, 70'. He may say that it means that my ability is such that the task, resigning, if it is not by choice, is a task that I cannot do, and that this entails that it is such that the task, resigning, if it is a task that I can do, is resigning by choice. But he cannot treat this pseudo exactly like the pseudo about the van, because choosing, in relation to resigning, is not an *S*-factor, and so this pseudo does not give the measure of my ability to resign, but, rather, offers an *a priori* truth about anybody's ability to resign. However, it does entail a statement in which the subordinate phrase has been contraposed. So though it does not entail its main contrapositive, it does entail its subordinate contrapositive.

This puts us in a position to explain the divergence of Austin's

two tests in this case. They diverge, because the tester's unavoidable verdict is that the hypothetical fails the contrapositive
test. He does not first choose to attach the antecedent to the
subordinate verb, and then decide that the hypothetical is a
pseudo which, like 'This van cannot do, if it is loaded, 70', does
not really have a contrapositive or a detached consequent. At
this stage he has to say that the detached consequent is 'I cannot
resign', which is not entailed by the original hypothetical. Hence
the divergence.

However, we can mitigate the paradox of this divergence by
making two explanatory points. First, since choosing is a
logically necessary adjunct of resigning, it would be natural if
the tester's first move were to attach the antecedent to the subordinate verb. Secondly, if he does make the attachment,
Austin's two tests do give the same result for the subordinate
phrase: we may replace it by its contrapositive, and we may not
replace it by its detached consequent. So it seems that this queer
case of divergence is produced by an unusual combination of
circumstances. First, the hypothetical cannot be taken in a way
that allows it to pass the contrapositive test. Secondly, in spite
of this, there is a reason for immediately attaching the antecedent to the subordinate verb, and then applying both Austin's
tests to the subordinate phrase. But thirdly, this reason is not
very easy to perceive, because it involves the special relationship
between resigning and choosing. What strikes us immediately
is the failure to pass the contrapositive test, and then our course
is set for the correct, but paradoxical, conclusion that the two
tests diverge in this case.

Integrated pseudos seem to be a fairly homogeneous class.
But it is likely that non-integrated pseudos will exhibit more
variety. Examples of non-integrated pseudos are 'There are
biscuits on the sideboard if you want them', and 'He can run a
mile in five minutes if you are interested'. In neither of these
cases does the antecedent govern the complementary verb—in
the first case for the best possible reason, that there is no complementary verb. In both cases the antecedent is in some way
attached to the passing of the message rather than to anything
said in the message. Hence the lack of integration. But this explanation of the lack of integration is unlikely to work for all non-
integrated pseudos. For example, Austin treats hypotheticals

like 'I can pay you tomorrow if I choose' as non-integrated pseudos[18] and, though I shall attempt to show that in fact they are integrated, Austin may be right, and yet in such cases the antecedent is certainly not attached to the passing of the message as it is in 'He can run a mile in five minutes, if you are interested'.

I shall now try to show that the pseudo 'I can pay you tomorrow if I choose' is an integrated pseudo. But the attempt may not succeed. It must be remembered that the word 'if' need not always govern something inside the sentence. Sometimes, if it governs anything, what it governs will have to be supplied in thought. So there is no presumption that the integrated treatment must work.

Let me begin by asking what this pseudo means. I think that there is no doubt that it means, roughly, 'I can pay you tomorrow, and if I choose to I shall'. My not choosing is being put forward as the only thing that may stand between my unexercised ability and actual performance. To put this in another way, my choosing is being put forward as the only absent, or possibly absent, necessary part of the total sufficient condition of performance. This implies that I shall have the opportunity, and so that there will be nothing to prevent me from paying you tomorrow. However, there is an important limitation on this last implication: as I argued earlier, this pseudo is used in such a way that it is non-committal about the possibility that I may be unable to bring myself to pay you tomorrow. The implication is only that, apart from this possibility—i.e. so far as ordinary ability and opportunity go—I can ('all-in') pay you tomorrow. In this implication the word 'can' is not being expanded to its limit.

We may characterize the meaning of this pseudo more briefly by saying that my choosing is being put forward as the 'performance-gap'—a convenient abbreviation of the long phrase 'the only absent or possibly absent necessary part of the total sufficient condition of performance'. This way of characterizing its meaning is really a combination of two of Austin's semi-paraphrases:

'I can; *quaere* do I choose to?'

and   'I can; I have only to choose to.'[19]

---

[18] Op. cit., p. 160. He calls them 'loose-jointed'.   [19] Op. cit., p. 160.

The concept of a performance-gap is a familiar one. It is used in such sentences as 'The plane will arrive on time if there is no fog.' The only unusual thing about the hypothetical 'I can pay you tomorrow if I choose' is that the performance-gap is here introduced in the antecedent of a pseudo. Hence the natural tendency to suggest the paraphrase 'I can pay you tomorrow, and, if I choose to, I shall', which restores the performance-gap to its usual position in the antecedent of a straightforward conditional, mentioning performance in its consequent.

It might be objected that this natural paraphrase cannot be reconciled with the thesis that 'I can pay you tomorrow' entails, roughly, that, if I choose to pay you tomorrow I shall. For, if this thesis is accepted, the paraphrase will contain a pointless redundancy: first it says that I can, and then, quite needlessly, it adds something which simply follows from 'I can'.

The way to find an answer to this objection is to look more closely at the suggested entailment. It is inexact to say that 'I can pay you tomorrow' entails that, if I choose to, I shall. We must allow for possible lack of opportunity, and for possible lapses. Here it is the opportunity that is important. For the pseudo 'I can pay you tomorrow if I choose' says what I can do tomorrow, and so carries an implication about my opportunity tomorrow. The implication is that I shall have the opportunity, and this implication is secured in the way already explained by the addition of the antecedent 'If I choose'. My choosing is put forward as the performance-gap, thus indicating that, so far as ordinary ability and opportunity go, there will be nothing to prevent me from paying you tomorrow. So the sentence 'I can pay you tomorrow' does not entail 'If I choose to pay you to-morrow I shall' until the antecedent has been added. The antecedent fixes the strength of the implied claim, and it is only after this has been done that the sentence 'If I choose to pay you tomorrow I shall' is entailed. So the alleged redundancy disappears.

The appearance of redundancy was an illusion produced by imprecision about the strength of the implied claim. A general ascription of a capacity, like 'I can buy any painting in the world' does not entail that if I choose to, I shall. It is necessary to be more precise and to say that, if anything, it entails that if I choose to, and if I have the opportunity, I shall. On the other hand, 'I can pay you tomorrow if I choose' really does entail that 'If I choose to I shall'. But this is only because the antecedent 'if I choose' has been added to 'I can pay you tomorrow', thus producing a pseudo strong enough to carry the entailment.

Some confirmation of this account of the meaning of 'I can if I choose' may be found in conversational usage. *A* asks *B* 'Can you be there at 5.00 tomorrow?', and *B* answers 'I can'—an answer which undoubtedly conveys the message that he will be there. But how is the message conveyed? One explanation is that here the verb 'can' has a secondary meaning, 'manage' or 'succeed', with no hint of mere potentiality.[20] But the objections to this explanation might well lead us to try to apply Grice's theory of conversational implicature to *B*'s answer. We shall then get an explanation of this conversational phenomenon which connects it with the account just given of the pseudo 'I can pay you tomorrow if I choose', and so provides some confirmation of that account. For in a context in which *B* knows that *A* wants to discover whether he will do a particular thing, and in which *A* knows that *B* knows that *A* wants to discover this, *A* may merely ask whether *B* can do that thing, because *B* will be under an obligation to mention any performance-gap of which he is aware. So when *B* merely replies 'I can', *A* is justified in taking him to imply that he is not aware of any performance-gap. If *B* had regarded his choosing to be there as an absent or possibly absent necessary part of the total sufficient condition of performance, then he ought to have added '. . . if I choose'. So the message that *B* will be there at 5.00 is conveyed as a conversational implicature governed by the general rule that information of the kind that is being sought should be maximized. This rule will not apply in every context, but only in the kind of context that has been specified. It is not necessary to add 'if I choose' to 'I can' in all cases in which my choosing is in fact the performance-gap, any more than it is always necessary to add 'if there were a cat around' to 'There is just enough room to swing a cat' (Groucho Marx's example). In the context specified above, the theory of conversational implicature seems to provide a better explanation of the message that *B* will be there than

---

[20] This explanation is adopted by A. M. Honoré in 'Can and Can't', *Mind* (1964), and by I. Thalberg in 'Austin on Ability', in *Symposium on J. L. Austin*, ed. K. T. Fann (1969).

the theory that the verb 'can' has its alleged secondary meaning. But the generalization of the theory of conversational implicature to all other cases of this phenomenon presents considerable difficulties.

It is one thing to observe that the performance-gap is introduced in an unusual position when it is mentioned in the subordinate phrase 'pay you tomorrow if I choose'; it is quite another thing to establish that this phrase is really a subordinate conditional. If this could be established, it would introduce some heterogeneity into the class of integrated pseudos. For in the present case the specificatory consecutive clause is 'such that, if I choose to pay you tomorrow, I *shall*', whereas, in the case examined earlier it was 'such that the task, doing 70, if the task is 70 without a load, is one which it *can* perform'. But can the theory of subordinate conditionals be extended to the present case?

Now there is no difficulty in showing that the sentence 'My capacity is such that, if I choose to pay you tomorrow, I shall' entails the sentence 'My capacity is such that, if I do not pay you tomorrow, I shall not have chosen to', in which the subordinate conditional has been contraposed. The difficult thing is to explain how, if at all, this subordinate conditional falls within the scope of the main verb 'can' in the original pseudo. Austin may have been right to treat it as a non-integrated pseudo.

The difficulty is connected with the difference between the consequents in the two consecutive clauses. It is all very well to say that the verbs in the two consequents are different—'shall pay' in the present case, and 'can perform' in the earlier case— and to observe that this difference would introduce some heterogeneity into the class of integrated pseudos. But is there not a fundamental difficulty here? For if 'I can pay you tomorrow if I choose' entails 'If I choose to pay you tomorrow, I shall', then 'I can pay you tomorrow' ought to entail 'I shall pay you tomorrow'. But 'I can pay you tomorrow' obviously does not entail 'I shall pay you tomorrow'. It carries this implication only as a conversational implicature in a special kind of context.[21]

The solution to this problem seems to lie in the peculiar function of the antecedent 'if I choose' in the pseudo 'I can pay

[21] This difficulty was pointed out by Paul Grice in discussion.

you tomorrow if I choose'. Its function here is to fix the strength
of the implied claim about what will be open to me tomorrow.
'I can pay you tomorrow' without the addition of this antecedent does not entail, even roughly, 'If I choose to pay you
tomorrow, I shall'. It is only when the antecedent has been
added that it carries the entailment. But from this it does not
follow that you can remove the antecedent 'If I choose' both
from the entailing statement, 'I can', and from the entailed
statement 'I shall', as is done by the objector. For the function
of the antecedent on the left-hand side of the entailment sign is
quite different from its function on the right-hand side of it. On
the left-hand side it is the antecedent of a pseudo, and its
function is to fix the strength of the implied claim about what
will be open to me tomorrow. But on the right-hand side it is
the antecedent of a conditional, and its function is to give the
sufficient condition of performance. Therefore the theory that
'I can if I choose' is an integrated pseudo is not open to the
objection that in that case 'I can pay you tomorrow' would
entail 'I shall pay you tomorrow'.

There might still be a complaint that the lack of homogeneity
in the class of integrated pseudos is a weakness in the theory.[22]
But there is no presumption that the verbs in the consequents
of the two consecutive clauses ought to be the same. Moreover,
the theory is capable of explaining the fact that they are different. So there is nothing arbitrary about the suggestion that
'This van can do 70 if it is unloaded' should be paraphrased as
'This van has a power such that the task, doing 70, if the task is
doing 70 without a load, is one which it can perform', whereas
'I can pay you tomorrow if I choose' should be paraphrased as
'My capacity is such that, if I choose to pay you tomorrow, I
shall'. The explanation of this difference is that the first pseudo
is a general ascription of power to the van, which, therefore,
introduces an S-factor in its antecedent, but no I-factor: whereas
the second pseudo does not put any limitation on my capacity
to pay you tomorrow, but, on the contrary, assesses it as high
enough to match tomorrow's opportunity, and, therefore, introduces an I-factor in its antecedent, but no S-factor. As I pointed
out earlier, it is possible to rewrite the first paraphrase as 'This

---

[22] A simpler theory would be preferable, if it fitted all the facts. But I cannot
think of one.

van has a power such that the task, doing 70, if the task is doing 70 without a load, and if it is driven with the throttle fully open, is one which it will perform'. This exhibits the relationship between the two species of integrated pseudo, but, naturally, it does not remove the differences between them.

It might still be objected that choosing is not really an *I*-factor, like depressing the accelerator of a van. But the answer to this objection is that the dissimilarities do not affect the similarity which justifies the classification of both as *I*-factors. Certainly, choosing is not always, or even typically, an event that is separate from the action. But the thesis that it is an *I*-factor does not require that it should be. It only requires that, if the claim implied by 'I can' is that, as far as ordinary ability and opportunity go, there is nothing to prevent me, then 'I can' entails, roughly, 'If I choose to, I shall' ('roughly', because there is many a slip between choosing and doing: strictly speaking, what is entailed is only a probability statement). So there is no implication about the categorization of choosing, which may even be in many cases a sort of adverbial qualification of the action itself. In general, the classification of factors as *I* or *S* is correlated with and only with the semantics of the hypotheticals in whose antecedents they are introduced.[23]

I would conclude that 'I can pay you tomorrow if I choose' is an integrated pseudo, introducing an *I*-factor in its antecedent, and thereby implying that this *I*-factor is the performance-gap. This would not be an isolated suggestion about 'I can if I choose'. It could be generalized to apply to cases in which the performance-gap is not an *I*-factor, but a stimulus linked to an *I*-factor: e.g. 'This rocket is programmed to shut down its engines if it reaches 90,000 feet', or 'He is prepared to hit you if you insult him'.

However, it must be observed that the pseudo 'I can pay you tomorrow if I choose' might introduce an *I*-factor in its antecedent, thereby implying that this *I*-factor is the performance-gap, *without* being integrated. That is, if Austin's view about its structure were correct, the remainder of my account would still apply to it. In that case, I could still claim that the antecedent governs the supplied consequent 'I shall'. But since this

[23] This general thesis runs up against some difficult cases, which will be discussed in Part II.

consequent is not in the sentence, there would be another alternative available—to interpret the 'if' as a wholly non-conditional 'if'. I shall not investigate this last alternative. The drive behind Part I of this paper has been the desire to extend the unified theory of conditional 'if' as far as possible. If it has been extended too far, that will not affect my classification of factors as I and S, or the correlation of this classification with the semantics of the hypotheticals in which they are introduced. The only difference will be that, because 'I can if I choose' will be interpreted as a non-integrated pseudo containing a non-conditional 'if', a different account will have to be given of the way in which my choosing is introduced as the performance-gap. It is in fact difficult to see how this different account would go. Yet it seems certain that my choosing is introduced as the performance-gap. Perhaps this provides additional confirmation that, even if 'I can if I choose' is a non-integrated pseudo, the 'if' in it is still a conditional 'if'.

II

The dispositional analysis of sentences ascribing powers and abilities to things and people runs into many difficulties. The situation is especially complex and confusing when such ascriptions are brought to bear on particular occasions, and carry some implication about the opportunities available on those occasions. Some of these difficulties are produced by superficial confusions, but I shall concentrate on those that beset any version of the dispositional analysis. Three difficulties will be examined, one presented by Lehrer, and two by Austin.

Lehrer presents his difficulty as a refutation of Moore's dispositional analysis of 'X could have acted otherwise', which was 'If X had chosen, he would have acted otherwise'.[24] I shall introduce his objection by relating it to the distinctions drawn in Part I. Expressed in my terminology, his point is that Moore's analysis presupposes that choosing is not an S-factor, and yet it might conceivably be an S-factor. From this he deduces that it might conceivably be the case that, since X did not choose to act otherwise (this is implied by the *analysandum*), he could not have acted otherwise, in spite of the truth of

[24] Lehrer, loc. cit.

Moore's *analysans*, that, if he had so chosen, he would have acted otherwise. For if choosing were an *S*-factor, it could be regarded as a necessary condition of *X*'s ability to act otherwise: i.e. it would be possible to interpret the hypothetical '*X* could not have acted otherwise unless he had chosen to' as a conditional. Lehrer's conclusion is that Moore's analysis should be rejected, because the *analysandum* might conceivably be false in spite of the truth of the *analysans*.

This objection may be expressed in the symbolism introduced in Part I. It is an objection to the thesis that *If Q then R* entails *P*. Now there may be other objections to this thesis, but for the time being I shall concentrate on this one. Bruce Aune has shown[25] that it is related to a much more widely used objection to Moore's analysis.[26] According to Lehrer's argument, the following triad is consistent:

(1) Moore's *analysans*.
(2) '*X* could not have acted otherwise unless he had chosen to' (interpreted counter-intuitively as a conditional).
(3) '*X* did not choose to act otherwise.'

According to the more widely used argument, the following triad is consistent:

(1) Moore's *analysans*.
(2) '*X* could not have acted otherwise unless he could have chosen (brought himself) to act otherwise.'
(3) *X* could not have chosen (brought himself) to act otherwise.'

The objection based on the consistency of the second triad was discussed briefly in Part I. It is, of course, connected with the more difficult part of the problem of determinism. It certainly points toward something important, but it does not refute Moore's analysis of ascriptions of ordinary ability and opportunity. The objection based on the consistency of the first triad will now be examined.

But first it is necessary to say something more about the distinction between *S*-factors and *I*-factors, because this distinction

---

[25] 'Hypotheticals and Can, another look', *Analysis* (1968). See also Lehrer's rejoinder 'Cans without ifs', ibid., and Aune's 'Reply to Lehrer', ibid. (1970).
[26] See Chisholm, loc. cit.

is relevant to the disagreement between Lehrer and Moore. It was presented in Part I as if it could never happen that a single factor could ever belong to both types. But that was only because simple examples were being used in order to get the distinction demarcated, and its general connection with the distinction between conditionals and pseudos established. So nearly all the factors considered were either S or I but not both. However, there are cases in which the factors introduced in the antecedents of hypotheticals, which have 'can' as the main verb of their consequents, fall under both concepts, I and S. These cases must now be examined, because the theory put forward in Part I ought to be capable of explaining them too, and because they throw some light on the disagreement between Lehrer and Moore.

One case of a factor which is both I and S was mentioned in Part I—the rather unusual case in which choosing is introduced as an S-factor after 'I can . . .', because the complementary verb leaves it open whether the action is to be done by choice or not. The example was 'I can shed tears if I choose', which was contrasted with 'I can resign if I choose'. In the first of these two cases, choosing might be an S-factor—for example the hypothetical might be uttered by an actor who might even be unable to shed tears naturally. In the second case, choosing is is not an S-factor, because it is already included in the concept of resigning, and so cannot be meant as a further specification of that performance. The point that needs to be added now is that in the first case, in which choosing is an S-factor, it will still retain its usual I character. It will therefore be an I- and S-factor.

This may seem unacceptable for two distinct reasons. First, choosing in 'I can . . . if I choose' nearly always functions as a pure I-factor. Secondly, it might be thought that, if it did simultaneously function as an S-factor, it would have to be regarded as something which gave the agent the capacity by bringing about some change in him: but Moore was quite right when he assumed that we do not regard choosing in this way; therefore, choosing cannot ever function as an S-factor.

But neither of these two arguments destroys the suggestion that choosing is sometimes an I- and S-factor. Against the first, it is enough to observe that the exceptional can happen, in this case explicably. The second argument is more interesting, but it is based on a mistaken assumption. For it is a mistake to assume that choosing could function as an *S*-factor only if it gave the agent the capacity by bringing about some change in him. It could equally well give him the capacity by 'bringing about some change' in the performance. In the example that is being considered, when the performance is shedding tears naturally, the actor lacks the capacity to shed them; but when it is shedding them by choice he has the capacity to shed them. This difference may be described as 'a change in the performance', but perhaps it is better to characterize it, as I did in Part I, by saying that the *S*-factor, choosing, is added as a further specification of the performance. Compare 'I could reach that book if it were two feet lower'.

There is, however, a more troublesome objection to the suggestion that choosing may sometimes be an *I*- and *S*-factor. It might be admitted that it could function as an *S*-factor in the exceptional cases described, but denied that it could simultaneously function as an *I*-factor. For it might seem impossibly strained for a speaker to introduce it once only in the antecedent of a hypothetical in order to make the two, quite different, points, that it is enough to bring the task, shedding tears, down within reach of his capacity, and that it is the performance-gap. Moreover, if anyone did introduce it with these two functions, *S* and *I*, the theory that has been put forward here could not be applied to the hypothetical. For, according to that theory, the hypothetical 'I can shed tears if I choose', has to be interpreted as a pseudo when choosing is an *I*-factor, and may be interpreted as a conditional when it is an *S*-factor. So, when choosing is an *I*- and *S*-factor, the theory could not be applied to the hypothetical without generating a contradiction.

But there seems to be a way of avoiding the contradiction without abandoning the theory. The paraphrase of 'I can if I choose' may be refined in order to accommodate this special case. Let us use the letters *I* and *S* as subscripts under the verbs in the antecedents of hypotheticals of this kind. Then the two functions of the factor introduced in the antecedent of 'I can if I choose' may be exhibited in the following, more elaborate paraphrase: 'If I choose$_S$, I can . . .' (this part may be interpreted as a main conditional) '. . . shed tears if I choose$_I$' (this part must be interpreted as a subordinate conditional if this antecedent is integrated into the structure of the sentence).

Naturally, the verb 'choose' appears twice in this paraphrase, because it has the two different functions indicated by the two subscripts. This is perfectly all right. However, this feature of the paraphrase will remind us that the residue of the objection —that it would be intolerably strained for the speaker to introduce choosing once only in order to make the two distinct points—remains unanswered. Would it be intolerably strained?

Perhaps the best way to answer this question would be to look at some other, less unusual, examples. But, first, the following tentative conclusions may be drawn from the hypothetical about the actor.

(1) If choosing is already included in the meaning of the verb of action, it cannot be an S-factor, and must be a pure I-factor.

(2) When choosing is an S-factor, it still retains its I-character, and so may be introduced to make two points simultaneously—that it is sufficient to bring the task down within reach of the subject's power, and that it is the performance-gap.

(3) In such a case, if we focus on its S-function, we may construe the hypothetical as a conditional, but from this it does not follow that we must regard choosing$_S$ as something which gives the agent the capacity by bringing about a change in him.

Anyone who reads Lehrer's objection to Moore's analysis of 'X could have acted otherwise' will immediately be struck by the importance of the first of these three points. But this point alone is not a sufficient basis for an answer to Lehrer, because choosing is not always included in the meaning of the verb of action.

Let me now take up the question whether there are any parallel examples, less unusual than the hypothetical about the actor, in which the speaker introduces a factor once and once only with the two different functions, I and S. The verb 'try', which is, incidentally, a more effective I-factor, provides the most convincing examples. For this verb means, roughly, 'attempt', and sometimes includes the additional meaning 'make an effort'. So if someone says 'I can solve this problem if I try', he might mean that he could solve it if he made an effort (a real effort), and in that case the factor introduced in the antecedent would have the two distinct functions. The two messages would then be that an effort would be sufficient to bring the task down within reach of his ability, and that an effort is the performance-gap. The elaborate paraphrase, with the two subscripts, I and S, under the verb-phrase 'make an effort', would exhibit the two functions of the factor that it designates. There is nothing mysterious about the message that making an effort$_I$ is the performance-gap. The point is that for this agent it is the appropriate kind of attempt, because making an effort$_S$ is needed as an additional specification of the task. The more usual case would be one in which attempting (without the extra qualification) could be put forward as a pure I-factor which is simply the performance-gap.

This example suggests a further development of the theory of factors. It is possible that in this case, when we focus on the S-function of making an effort, we might regard it as something which gives the agent the ability by bringing about a change in him.[27] If it is a fact that we could regard it in this way, it is an important fact. For it would provide us with an example of an ordinary pre-action verb (i.e. a verb like 'choose' and 'want', which takes the agent as subject) which produces two effects in the agent: first, it gives him the ability by bringing about a change in him, and then it activates this newly bestowed ability. The suggestion that making an effort might be regarded in this way, which goes beyond the thesis that it has an S-function (see point (3)), is obviously relevant to the disagreement between Lehrer and Moore.

Is the suggestion correct? It is difficult to answer this question, partly because the answer would need to be based on the neurophysiology of making an effort, which would presumably differ from case to case. But for my purpose it is sufficient to provide a general *schema* for answering it.[28] The general answer is that making an effort may be regarded as a factor which produces a capacity in a subject by bringing about a change in that

[27] This possibility was suggested by Philippa Foot in discussion.
[28] The argument that follows is a development of a suggestion made by George Myro in discussion.

subject, and which also activates that capacity. But if a single factor is to have these two functions, it must have two distinct aspects, each connected with one of the two functions in a way that, ideally, ought to be intelligible. Otherwise, when we attributed the two functions to the factor, we would, in effect, be postulating two capacities where there is really only an adequate basis for one. If the requirement is not met, there is only an adequate basis for the capacity to achieve performance *A*, and so what we ought to say is that, *so far as changes in the subject go*, the factor is only an *I*-factor which produces performance *A*. If we also regard it as an *S*-factor, we cannot regard it as an *S*-factor which gives the subject the capacity to do *A* by bringing about a change in him. If we claimed that this same factor, with no difference of aspect, is not only an *I*-factor but also an *S*-factor which gives him the capacity to do *A* by bringing about a change in him, we would be postulating a second capacity in the subject, the capacity to achieve the capacity to do *A*, without an adequate basis in fact or theory. That would be like maintaining that the space occupied, as we now say, by one material object, e.g. a table, is really occupied by two indiscernible tables. This would violate the principle of counting material objects, and similarly the attribution of a second capacity to the subject, when the requirement was not met, would violate the principle of counting capacities.

It is, as I said, difficult to answer the question whether making an effort meets the requirement that it should have two distinct aspects. A case in which the requirement is clearly met is provided by the following mechanical example: someone manufactures a car in which the accelerator-pedal starts the engine with the first part of its angular movement, and also continuously opens the throttle in the usual way. In this case the factor, depressing the pedal to a certain point, does meet the requirement, and so may be regarded both as an *S*-factor which gives the car a certain power by bringing about a change in it, and as an *I*-factor which activates this newly bestowed power.

It might be thought that the imposition of this requirement contradicts something that was said earlier. For in a hypothetical like 'I could reach that book if it were two feet lower', the factor introduced in the antecedent was said to be an *S*-factor, and so the hypothetical was said to be interpretable as a conditional, meaning that the S-factor would give me the ability to reach the book. But making an effort was also said to be something that the agent does, and so, presumably, like other actions, something that he is capable of doing. It seems to follow that making an effort might be regarded as something which gives him the capacity to solve the problem by bringing about a change in him, even if the requirement is not met. But the apparent contradiction vanishes if we distinguish between the statement that a factor is something that happens in a subject and the statement that, when it happens, it brings about a change in the subject and in this way gives him the capacity. It is indisputable that making an effort is a factor which may be characterized in the first of these two ways, and that is all that follows from what was said earlier. It is a debatable question whether it should also be characterized in the second way, and there is no contradiction in maintaining that an affirmative answer cannot be given to this question unless the requirement is met. But even if the requirement is not met, making an effort may still be an S-factor.

So it seems legitimate to add a fourth point to the previous three:

(4) When an S-factor is also an I-factor, it cannot be regarded as something which gives the subject a capacity by bringing about a change in the subject, unless the following requirement is met: the factor must have two distinguishable aspects, each connected, preferably in an intelligible way, with one of its two effects.

The theory of factors, with these additions and qualifications, may now be applied to Lehrer's objection to Moore's analysis of 'X could have done otherwise'.

Lehrer's objection is based on the suggestion that it might conceivably be true that X could not have acted otherwise unless he had chosen to. It is superficial, but worth while, to make the point that this hypothetical is naturally taken as a pseudo, meaning that X could not have acted otherwise without choosing to; in which case, as was pointed out earlier, if acting otherwise is specified in a way that includes choosing in its meaning, it would be an understatement to say that the hypothetical might conceivably be true, because it would be true *a priori*. But of course Lehrer is suggesting that choosing might conceivably be an *S*-factor, and that the hypothetical might conceivably be a contingently true conditional.

One way of understanding this suggestion is the way that was appropriate to the hypothetical about the actor. That is, we only need to suppose that acting otherwise is not specified in a way that includes choosing in its meaning, and then it is easy to accept the suggestion that choosing might be an *S*-factor, and that the hypothetical might be a contingently true conditional. Notice that the acceptance of this suggestion would not commit us to the counter-intuitive idea that choosing would be an *S*-factor which would give the agent the capacity by bringing about a change in him. However, again it is obvious that this is not Lehrer's interpretation of the hypothetical. For his objection to Moore's analysis is offered as an entirely general one, which is not confined to cases explicable in the special way appropriate to the hypothetical about the actor. He really is suggesting that, quite generally, choosing might be an *S*-factor, and—what is more—an *S*-factor which, by bringing about a change in the agent, produces in him, as nothing else does, the capacity to do *A*.

So his suggestion raises the question whether the requirement in point (4) is in fact met by choosing. But, before this question is tackled, it would be as well to take a broader look at his strategy, and at the obstacles to its success. His strategy is to argue that his hypothetical might conceivably be true in the way just specified at a moment when it was also true that *X* did not choose to act otherwise. It would follow that at that moment *X* could not have acted otherwise, in spite of the fact that Moore's *analysans* '*X* would have acted otherwise if he had chosen to' might well be true.

One obstacle to the success of this strategy is that the hypotheticals 'I can resign if I choose to' and 'I cannot resign if I do not choose to' are not in fact used in this way. This obstacle is not made less formidable by its superficiality. For when Lehrer deduces from the second and third members of his triad that at that moment *X* could not have acted otherwise, a defender of Moore's analysis may reply with a dilemma: either this proposition does not have the same meaning as the negation of the *analysandum*, or else the two premises are not consistent with

Moore's *analysans*, which is the first member of the triad.[29] The second horn of this dilemma is likely to provoke the dogged assertion that the triad really is consistent, and then this part of the controversy will have reached an impasse of the same tedious kind that Moore himself reached in one of his arguments with ethical naturalists in *Principia Ethica*. But the first horn of the dilemma needs closer scrutiny. What, if anything, is the difference between the meaning of the proposition which Lehrer deduces from the second and third members of his triad and the negation of Moore's *analysandum*?

To deny Moore's *analysandum* is to deny that X had the ability and opportunity to act otherwise. The proposition which Lehrer deduces from the second and third members of his triad seems at first sight to have precisely the same meaning as this denial. But, if Moore is right, the two propositions differ in meaning—indeed, according to him, they necessarily differ in meaning, if the triad is consistent (i.e. according to him, the first horn of the dilemma must be rejectible if its second horn is not rejectible). Moore takes this view because he retains the fundamental assumption which we all make in this matter—that choosing is a pure I-factor, or else, occasionally, not only an I-factor, but also an S-factor, which, because it does not meet the requirement in point (4), cannot give the agent the capacity by bringing about a change in him. This is the rationale supporting his claim that his *analysans* entails his *analysandum*. Lehrer, on the other hand, is suggesting that our fundamental assumption may be mistaken, in which case, as we have seen, choosing would have to be an S-factor which met the requirement in point (4). This is the rationale supporting his counter-claim that Moore's *analysans* does not entail his *analysandum*. But, as Aune has shown,[30] Moore would not have to defend his analysis by arguing that the assumption which supports it could not conceivably be mistaken. The superficial point, that in fact we make the assumption on that basis, and use the *analysandum* with the meaning that he ascribes to it, is a sufficient defence of his analysis. He only has to show that, against the background of things as they are—or,

---

[29] This reply is very effectively developed by Bruce Aune in his two criticisms of Lehrer, 'Hypotheticals aud Can, another look', *Analysis* (1968), and 'Reply to Lehrer', ibid. (1970).

[30] Locc. citt.

rather, as we assume that they are—we treat the hypothesis, that his *analysans* might be true, without the *analysandum* being true, as inconceivable. He does not carry the additional onus of proving that it is inconceivable that we should ever reject the assumption, and, as a result, treat the hypothesis as conceivable. No analysis *has* to be defended in that way.

This point may be reinforced by asking what characterization of the agent would be projectible into the intervals between his choices, if our fundamental assumptions about choosing turned out to be mistaken. The answer which involves the smallest change in our conceptual scheme is that, instead of projecting the ability to do *A*, as Moore rightly claims that we do, we would start projecting the ability to achieve the ability to do *A*. For choosing would be regarded as a factor which gave the agent the ability to do *A* by bringing about a change in him (*S*-function), and then immediately activated it (*I*-function). Moore can hardly be criticized for not anticipating this new usage with his analysis.

In practice the change introduced by the new usage would be small. But from a theoretical standpoint, it would be large. For, as we have seen, the new conceptual scheme for choosing and ability would be viable only if choosing met the requirement in point (4)—that it be a factor with two distinguishable aspects, each connected, preferably in an intelligible way, with one of its two effects. It is not enough for the innovator to suggest that it might be a mistake to assume that choosing is either a pure *I*-factor or else occasionally not only an *I*-factor but also an *S*-factor which does not give the agent the ability to do *A* by bringing about a change in him. The innovator must add that it might be the case that choosing met the requirement in point (4).

Does choosing meet this requirement? This is a big question, and I do not see how it can be answered at present. For it seems to be a question which lies on the borderline of two incompletely explored fields, the conceptual analysis of pre-action verbs, like 'want', 'choose', and 'try', and their underlying neuro-physiology.

But, whatever the answer to that question, it is clear that there are faults in the strategy of Lehrer's objection to Moore's analysis of '*X* could have acted otherwise'. So I conclude that his objection to this particular thesis of the form '*If Q then R entails P*' is invalid. Of course, it does not follow from this that there are no valid objections to theses of this form.

Austin, in fact, makes a suggestion which might be used as a basis for criticizing theses of this form from a different angle. He is examining Nowell-Smith's version of the dispositional analysis of the general ascription of ability '*X* can do *A*', which is 'If *X* has the opportunity to do *A*, and a preponderant motive for doing it, he will do it.'[31] Austin applies this to the example 'Smith can run a mile', and he observes that in this case, though it is true that *P* follows from *If Q then R*, the antecedent *If Q* is redundant, because *P* follows from *R* alone.[32] It is not clear how far he is prepared to generalize this suggestion, because he also remarks that there are good reasons for not saying that 'I can lift my finger' is directly verified when I proceed to lift it.[33] But in a case in which the suggestion is valid, it seems that it could be used as the basis of a new criticism of theses of the form '*If Q then R* entails *P*'. For if *R* alone really does entail *P*, we could discard *If Q*, or keep it and give *Q* any value under the sun.

It seems that Austin's suggestion could also be used as a basis for criticizing theories of the form '*P* entails *If Q then R*'. M. R. Ayers puts it to this use in *The Refutation of Determinism*.[34] He

---

[31] *Ethics* (1952), chs. 19 and 20.

[32] Op. cit., p. 175.

[33] Op. cit., p. 171, footnote. Irving Thalberg argues that this footnote appears to contradict the passage on p. 175, and that the way to remove the contradiction is to observe that 'Smith will run a mile' entails 'Smith can run a mile' only because the verb 'can' here has its secondary meaning 'succeed', so that the two sentences mean the same ('Austin on Abilities', in *Symposium on J. L. Austin*, ed. K. T. Fann (1969), pp. 182 ff.). But it is not clear what point Austin is making in the footnote, and there is an alternative to Thalberg's remedy.

When Austin claims that *R* alone entails *P*, his claim can be defended without interpreting *P* as 'Smith succeeds in running a mile'. For Smith's running a mile proves that it is possible that he should run a mile, and since running a mile involves trying to do something which is at least closely related to running a mile, it also proves that he has the capacity to run a mile, even though the proof of this last statement requires the truth of *Q*. This is characteristic of cases in which we do not commonly need to draw the distinction between doing *A* as the full action *A*, and doing *A* not as the full action *A*.

This explanation will be developed in what follows. Thalberg's explanation, that the verb 'can' here has its secondary meaning 'succeed', will not be discussed. It would need to be worked out in detail, and pitted against the rival theory that, when there is an implication of success, it can be explained as a conversational implicature.

[34] pp. 125–35.

argues that, if the entailment really did hold in this direction, then anything that was evidence for P would also be evidence for *If Q then R*. But the truth of R alone is evidence for P without being evidence for *If Q then R*. Therefore, P does not entail *If Q then R*. He appears to use this argument quite generally, and not to mark any restriction on the validity of Austin's suggestion.

The two criticisms both use Austin's suggestion as a basis, and the second one is also based on the further assumption that *If Q then R* is something more than a material implication. In fact Austin does not develop the criticism of theses of the form '*If Q then R entails P*'. But Ayers does develop the related criticism of theses of the form '*P entails If Q then R*'. I shall now examine the basis that is common to both criticisms. I shall not give Q the rather complex value that Nowell-Smith gives it, nor even the value 'he chooses', which I gave it earlier. For even when a person can do a thing, there is many a slip between the I-factors wanting and choosing and actual performance. I shall, therefore, give Q the value 'he tries', so that the I-factor introduced by *If Q* will be a more effective one. Also, in order to simplify the discussion that follows, I shall assume that the opportunity is perfect. These tactical conventions will not affect the main issue in this controversy.

Is Austin's suggestion, that R alone entails P, correct? That seems to depend on the kind of performance that is in question. 'Smith can run a mile' really does seem to be entailed by 'Smith has just run a mile'. But, by way of contrast, suppose that P is 'X can hit a bull's-eye with a .22 rifle at 150 yards'. In this case it is easy to imagine situations in which R is true, Q is false and P is not established. For example, X shuts his eyes and sweeps the rifle round in a series of random arcs, and while he is doing this squeezes the trigger, and hits the bull's-eye 150 yards away. This does not establish that he has the ability ascribed to him by P. It only establishes that it is possible that he (or anyone else) should hit a bull's-eye (or anything else) 150 yards away, because an object at that distance is within the range of a .22 rifle, and, if it is not behind cover, may be hit. What is lacking in this case is the truth of Q: he was not trying to hit the bull's-eye.

It is true that in this case there would also be something else wrong with the claim that the truth of R established P. For, whatever counts as success, one success is usually not enough to support the ascription of a capacity or ability to a person.[35] But, though this deficiency is important, it does not detract from the importance of the other deficiency that has just been noted in this way of trying to establish *P*. For suppose that we multiply the instances of the truth of *R* without the truth of *Q*: i.e. *X* repeats his movements with his eyes shut again and again, and very often gets the same amazing result. We would then decide that more was being established than that it was merely possible to hit something at 150 yards with a .22 rifle. At the very least it would begin to look probable that the target assigned to *X* before he shut his eyes would be hit.

But this is not the only conclusion that could be drawn from these surprising facts. We might put forward the more ambitious hypothesis that *X* had a remarkable gift which made the usual fussy style of marksmanship unnecessary. This hypothesis could be tested in other places, and with other rifles, and it might be confirmed. If so, *X* would be credited with a new ability, the ability to hit targets without squinting down the sights of his rifle, and, when *P* was given this new value, it might seem that it really would be established by repeated instances of the truth of *R* without the truth of *Q*.

However, this would be an illusion. It is, no doubt, likely that in the circumstances *X* would be credited with a new ability. But if this conclusion were drawn from the facts, his new technique—shutting his eyes and the rest—would have become for him another way of trying to hit the target. He would be like a person who begins by trying to predict future events in the usual inductive way, collecting and assessing evidence, but then discovers that what he sees in a crystal ball always happens later: looking into a crystal ball would soon become for such a person another way of trying to predict future events. Similarly, *X* would have replaced the old technique of marksmanship with a new one. During the transition the antecedent *If Q* may seem to drop out as irrelevant, but in fact, if *P* is going to remain the ascription of an ability, the old value of *Q* must be replaced by a new one.

It hardly matters in this case whether we would think that we

---

[35] Thalberg makes this point about rifle-shooting, and also the related point that different abilities require characteristically different success-rates. Op. cit., pp. 187 ff.

were also giving P a different value, or whether we would regard the ability ascribed to X after the transition as the same old ability based on a new technique. The important point is that we cannot expel the antecedent while P remains the ascription of an ability. This reveals the logical structure of ascriptions of abilities to persons. It was claimed in Part I that such an ascription means more than that the performance is consistent with all known facts and laws. For its truth requires that there should be an identifiable I-factor, given which (and given, as I am now assuming, the opportunity), the performance will ensue, or, at least, will ensue in a high enough proportion of cases. Some confirmation of this claim can be extracted from the present discussion. For I am arguing against a suggestion which serves as the basis of a criticism both of the thesis that P entails *If Q then R*, and of the thesis that *If Q then R* entails P. The suggestion is that the truth of R alone is sufficient to establish P. But this suggestion misleadingly discards the increment of meaning which is essential to ascriptions of abilities to people, because it distinguishes them not only from statements beginning 'It is possible that . . .' but also from statements beginning 'It is probable that . . .' The increment contributed by the antecedent *If Q* will be the requirement that there should be a definite technique, as in the present example, or else basic trying, as it would be if P were 'He can move his ears'. Naturally, this does not imply that there is no other characteristic difference between the meaning of an ascription of an ability to a person and the other two types of statement.

It is interesting to observe how the two deficiencies in the original method of establishing 'He can hit a bull's-eye with a .22 rifle at 150 yards' co-operate with one another. At first, when X had only done it once with his eyes shut, the evidence for ascribing the ability to him was inadequate in both ways; it was the wrong kind of instance, and it was only a single instance. So all that was established at this point was a statement beginning 'It is possible that . . .' When the instances were multiplied with frequent success, the inference was a statement beginning 'It is probable that . . .' At this point there was a choice in the telling of the story and the final conclusion would depend on what happened next—i.e. on the type of case in which experiment discovered a high rate of success. It might have turned out that it did not make any difference who spun the rifle, and that it was not even necessary that it should be spun by a person, but that it had to be that particular rifle. In that case a mysterious power would be ascribed to the rifle, and the ascription would entail a hypothetical mentioning a specific *I*-factor in its antecedent. But the story was developed in a way that was favourable to the ascription of an ability to *X*, and it emerged that it was essential to this development that *X* should come to regard his antics as a new technique for achieving the same performance, or, to put the point in a way that connects it with the theory of factors, that he should regard them as a new *I*-value for *Q* in the hypothetical *If Q then R*. In short, the ascription of an ability or power is an extract from the total situation —an extract which can be made only if the appropriate *I*-factor is there.

However, there are gaps in this account. Suppose that at the point where there was a choice in the development of the story, things had taken a different turn, and experiment had shown that *X* only needed to be near the rifle, and then, if it were spun and fired mechanically, the same score of bull's-eyes would be achieved. This seems to be a case in which we would not ascribe an ability to *X*, in spite of the fact that, if he placed himself near the rifle (verb of action), then given the opportunity (the mechanical rotation of the rifle), the bull's-eye would often be hit. What we would ascribe to *X* would be a usable power, based presumably on his physical properties.

It would be a lengthy business to explain this difference fully. The salient point seems to be that *X* would be using his body just like any other material object, so that it is unduly narrow to give *Q* the value 'he places himself near the rifle', which is a verb of action. What we ought to say is that *X*'s body has a certain power which manifests itself in the way specified provided that it is near the rifle (*I*-factor), and the rifle is rotated (opportunity). No doubt, this is a fantastic example, but it is easy to find everyday cases in which a power of this kind is ascribed to a person's body rather than an ability to the person. For example, an expert in acoustics might say that human bodies can absorb sound; or someone might say '*X* can sink a canoe', meaning that he can sink one by the mere weight of his body.

In general, given facts structured as they are in this last

development of the story, it is possible to ascribe either an ability to X, or to X's body the kind of physical power which is independent of the fact that X is a self-mover. Which of the two ascriptions we make will depend on the way in which X uses his body, if indeed he does use it. In the last case mentioned, if X did use his body to sink canoes, we might say that he sank them (verb of action), and we might also ascribe the corresponding ability to him. Evidently, the distinction between the proper evidence for an ascription of a power of this kind and the proper evidence for an ascription of an ability is not an exclusive distinction. A thorough investigation of it would lead far afield into the concepts of action, consequence, and skill, and would require a long discussion of different possible theoretical backgrounds.

There is also another gap in my argument against the thesis that in this kind of case the truth of R alone is enough to establish P. For when P is 'Smith can run a mile', it seems that the truth of R alone really is enough to establish P. So I have to explain what marks off this kind of example from the last one. This gap too would take a long time to fill adequately, but I can make a start.

The salient point here seems to be that we do not commonly need to distinguish between running a mile as a full human action and running a mile not as a full human action. For the verb of action 'run a mile' nearly always includes trying to run a mile, or, at least, trying to do something that is closely related to running a mile (cf. the parallel point about resigning and choosing in Part I). So when Smith actually runs a mile, we do not need to stipulate, as something extra, that he must be trying to run a mile, before allowing that it has been established that he has the ability or capacity to run a mile. The truth of R in this case, involves the truth of Q. So Austin's original suggestion about this example needs to be taken with some scepticism. It is true that here the verification of R alone is enough to establish P. But it is misleading to express this truth in this way, and a plain *suggestio falsi* if the point of expressing it in this way is to eliminate the antecedent *If Q*.

To put the same point in a different way, Smith may be lucky to run his mile, but his luck cannot be like the luck of a man who hits his target without even trying to hit it. On the rifle-range we do need to distinguish between hitting the target as a full human action and hitting it without even trying to hit it, and the second of these two performances does not support the ascription of an ability. But on the race-track we do not have to guard against the possibility of a performance of the second kind. For it is not possible for a runner to have the good luck to run a mile, when, for example, he thought that he was marking time, like a car with its engine running in neutral.

When this point was made earlier (p. 127 footnote 33), I said that the truth of Q makes the difference between a case of the truth of R which supports 'X has the ability' and a case of the truth of R which only supports 'It is possible that X should . . .' This is roughly correct, but it needs qualification in the light of the intervening discussion. For sometimes, when the truth of Q is not required, what is established will be that X's body has a power of the kind that is independent of the fact that he is a self-mover, rather than the non-ascriptive proposition that it is possible that X should . . . These seem to be cases in which Austin's suggestion is true, and not misleadingly expressed provided that it is only meant to exclude antecedents containing pre-action verbs like 'try'. But if it is also meant to exclude antecedents introducing other kinds of I-factor, then it is misleading. For powers like the power to sink a canoe by one's own weight involve factors which, though they are not designated by pre-action verbs like 'try', are none the less I. If we wish to find examples which do not involve I-factors, the best way to find them is to go all the way down to cases where the evidence only supports non-ascriptive statements of possibility. Perhaps there are also cases where the evidence supports non-ascriptive statements of probability but does not support any ascription of power or ability, but this is more doubtful.

It appears, then, that when P is an ascription of an ability, Austin's original suggestion, even when it is true, cannot be used as the basis of a criticism either of the thesis that P entails *If Q then R* or of the thesis that *If Q then R* entails P. A full development of the argument against these uses of it would involve a lengthy investigation of the concepts of ability and power. But perhaps two minor points may be added before this topic is left.

I have been arguing that, where P is the ascription of an ability to a person, the truth of R without the truth of Q is not sufficient to establish P, and that this is not merely because one confirmatory instance is not enough, but also because it is the wrong kind of instance. This is not the same as saying that, in order to establish P, we need to establish that the truth of Q is a necessary condition of the truth of R. That would be an absurd thing to say, because a person who has the ability to hit the bull's-eye at 150 yards with a .22 rifle may happen to do that very thing accidentally. As we have seen, an accidental performance is not enough to establish that he has the ability. But neither does it establish that he lacks the ability. To insist that the truth of R without the truth of Q is not sufficient to establish P is not the same thing as requiring that the truth of Q should be a necessary condition of the truth of R. In fact, the reason for insisting on the former point is precisely that in cases in which the I-factor introduced in *If Q* is not included in the meaning of the verb of action, R may be true without Q being true.

It might be objected that, though I am not saying that trying is a necessary condition of successful performance, I am saying that it is a necessary—in fact, a logically necessary—condition of the kind of successful performance that is required to support P, and this may seem to be incompatible with the thesis that it is a contingently sufficient condition of successful performance. But the appearance of incompatibility is an illusion. Someone might say that 'This is safety-glass' entails 'If it breaks, it breaks into tiny fragments'.[36]

As I said, Austin does not develop either of these two criticisms of Nowell-Smith's analysis of ascriptions of abilities to people. The criticism which he does develop is more damaging, but perhaps not so damaging as he takes it to be. It is developed in two closely related stages.[37] First, he points out that from the fact that P entails *If Q then R*, it does not follow that *If Q then R* entails P. Secondly, he argues that from the fact that, if P and Q are true, then R must be true, we cannot infer that P simply means that, if Q is true, R will be true. If this inference were valid, we could also argue that Q simply means that, if P is true, R will be true. But when P, Q, and R are given the values that they have been given here, this is absurd. According to him, these are not two different stages in the development of his

[36] An example used by M. R. Ayers, op. cit., p. 134.
[37] Austin, op. cit., pp. 173–7.

criticism, but simply two different ways of making the same point. But in fact we shall find that the second goes further than the first.

There are also some unimportant differences between the way in which he presents his criticism and the way in which it is being presented here. He mentions opportunity in his formula, but I have omitted it, on the assumption made earlier, that it is perfect. Also he gives Q the value 'he has a preponderant motive', but I am giving it the value 'he tries', because trying is a more effective I-factor. These differences will simplify the discussion of his criticism without affecting the main issue.

It can hardly be doubted that the point made in the first stage of his criticism is correct: the thesis, that P entails *If Q then R*, does not entail its converse. It is, therefore, invalid to argue in this way for the dispositional analysis of ascriptions of abilities or powers. The truth of the premiss of this argument would leave it an open possibility that such an ascription might mean more than *If Q then R*.

Perhaps it would be helpful to fill in some more details. From the premiss that P entails *If Q then R*, we really may infer that Q entails *If P then R*. Austin does not mention this, because his concern is to point out that neither the premiss of this inference nor its conclusion entails its converse. But it is worth mentioning because it provides some confirmation for the view that in each case the dispositional formula on the right-hand side does give at least part of the meaning of the proposition on the left-hand side. For, after inferring that Q entails *If P then R*, we may notice that, with the values already assigned, this conclusion seems to be true. It really does seem to be part of the meaning of 'He is trying to do A' that, if he has the ability, he will do A— or, at least, that he will do A in a sufficiently high proportion of cases in which his contribution to the outcome is the same.

Although the two converse statements do not follow from the direct statements, it is worth inquiring whether they are true. For if they were true, then, given the truth of the two direct statements, the dispositional formulae on the right-hand side would be complete analyses of P and Q respectively. Some philosophers have maintained that this is indeed the case with P, but they can hardly take the same line about Q, because, as was observed in Part I, at least one of the two propositions, P or

Q, will need sufficient conditions independent of the dispositional formula. Otherwise both dispositional formulae will be unusable. For example, we might want to use them in order to establish that X lacked the ability to do A, because, though he often tried, he always failed; but we would be unable to establish that he often tried, if our only resource was the two-way dispositional formula, that, if and only if he tries, then, if he has the ability, he will succeed. A single equation with two unknown quantities is insoluble. So at least one of the two propositions, P and Q, needs an independent sufficient condition, and certainly Q seems to have one. This feature of Q allows us to establish via the truth of Q that X has the ability to do A, and then on a particular occasion, when we doubt his claim that he really is trying to do A, we may rely on the truth of P and use the formula 'Q entails *If P then R*'. But then this independent sufficient condition has a claim to be included in the meaning of Q which is as strong as the claim of the dispositional formula. If there is also an independent sufficient condition of P, it too will have a claim to be included in the meaning of P which is as strong as the claim of the dispositional formula *If Q then R*.

This argument, though largely convincing, leaves much unexplained. We need a detailed account of the breakdown of the two converse statements '*If P then R* entails Q' and '*If Q then R* entails P', if indeed they do break down. Certainly, they do not follow from the direct statements, but this does not show that they are incorrect. However, the first is in fact incorrect, for a reason that has already been discussed. X may have the ability to do A and yet do it accidentally, and then it need not be true that he tried to do A: i.e. P and R may be true without Q being true.

The case against the converse statement, '*If Q then R* entails P' is more complex. Two points have already been made in this area. First, because P ascribes an ability, which has temporal spread, its verification requires repeated instances of the truth of Q and R. In this respect P is to be contrasted with Q, which reports an event and obviously does not require any repetition of instances for its verification. Secondly, when R is true in a sufficiently high proportion of cases of the truth of Q, that is enough to verify P. The second point now needs to be amplified and qualified. A lot was said about the fact that, for many values of P, instances of the truth of R that are favourable to the truth of P require the truth of Q. But there was no discussion of the related question, whether the general statement 'Whenever X tries to do A he succeeds' (or an appropriate statistical general statement) actually entails P. It is one thing to say that a run of instances favourable to this general statement is enough to verify P, but quite another thing to say that the general statement entails P. Transference of verification is a less exacting relation than entailment.

The reason why a qualification needs to be added is that X might try to do A, and do A, in spite of the fact that his attempt was totally inadequate. In such a case, the explanation of his success would be luck: he was aided by some unforeseen and perhaps unforeseeable factor. Now this might conceivably happen often and, if it did, he might become superstitious, and we might mistakenly ascribe the ability to him. The existence of this possibility is enough to show that the general hypothetical does not entail P. It is also necessary that X's trying should really produce his successes. The theoretical background must be right. This requirement is easily forgotten, because in cases where the success is repeated again and again we naturally take it for granted that the theoretical background is right, perhaps without even knowing what it is, and so hold that P has been verified.

This is a perfectly reasonable attitude in practice, particularly when the sequence of successes has been so prolonged that the alternative hypothesis would be a fantastic coincidence, but it does not justify the theory that the general hypothetical entails P. However, it might seem to justify the theory that P is more dispositional than Q. But this theory needs to be treated with caution, and even with some scepticism. For the extra element that has to be added to the general dispositional formula in order to produce a proposition that really does entail P is important, and its claim to be included in the meaning of P really does seem to be as strong, or, at least, nearly as strong, as the claim of the dispositional factor to which it is added. Moreover, the addition will usually amount to more than the stipulation that X did not achieve his successes by luck. His own contribution, which we call 'trying', ought to be seen to produce his successes in an appropriately direct way. For example, it

K

must not be the case that a demon always corrects his bungling attempts. But it is not enough that there should be no evidence that anything extraneous produced his successes. The extra requirement, in its most complete and satisfying form, will include an account of the structure of X and of the function of whatever is designated by the verb 'try' in the relevant instances.

It is easy to exaggerate this point in reaction against the excessive claims that have been made in the past for the dispositional analysis of ascriptions of powers and abilities to things and people. So it would be as well to cut it down to life-size. Although knowledge of the extra element is desirable, it is often lacking. We often simply do not know the theoretical basis of the performances, and yet in many cases of this kind we are justified in making the ascription. Moreover, in a case in which we can fill in the extra requirement, it will be an element in the meaning of P that is less important than the dispositional formula. For if the general hypothetical were repeatedly falsified in generously varied circumstances, it would simply be a mistake to maintain P on the ground that the subject satisfied the accepted theoretical requirement. In such a case we would reformulate the theoretical requirement because the dispositional formula always remains the dominant partner in this syndicate of meaning. So, though it would be an exaggeration to say that the dispositional formula entails P, it would be an even greater exaggeration to say that the other partner entails P. This, of course, raises the much discussed problem of multiple criteria. In what sense of 'sufficient' do we sometimes have a sufficient condition of P which is independent of the dispositional formula? This question needs to be answered by anyone who wants to assess the force of the earlier argument that either P or Q needs an independent sufficient condition which will have as strong a claim to be included in its meaning as the claim of the dispositional formula. But I shall not attempt to answer it.

Let us look, finally, at the suggestion that Q is less dispositional than P. There are several reasons for making this suggestion. First, it has already been pointed out that Q entails the singular hypothetical *If P then R*—or rather, since this has to be qualified to allow for cases of fallible ability, that at least it entails that if P is true, then R will be true in a sufficiently high proportion of cases. Naturally, the generality in this necessary condition of Q

does not involve temporal spread, because X's trying is a single event, even if the ascription of power to this event entails a general hypothetical. Incidentally, this characterization of trying presupposes that it is also characterized in another, non-dispositional, way. Otherwise it would be impossible to specify the cases in a high proportion of which R must be true. They must be specified as cases in which X's contribution to the outcome is the same again. However, the generality in the dispositional characterization of trying does not involve temporal spread, and this seems to be one of the considerations supporting the idea that Q is less dispositional than P. Another is that the converse thesis, that *If P then R* entails Q, breaks down for the reason mentioned earlier, that, even if X has the ability to do A, he may do it accidentally.

This raises the same question about Q that has just been answered for P: what more has to be added to the dispositional formula in order to produce a proposition which entails Q? Here two distinct but related extra elements are available: there is X's sincere report that he did try, and in certain cases there is physical evidence that he did try. If we lacked both these extra elements, we could not even bridge the gap between the verification of *If P then R* and the verification of Q. So these are not merely desirable but dispensable additions, like the extra element in the meaning of P. On the contrary, they are dominant partners in their syndicate of meaning, because they are sufficient to establish that X tried to do A even on those possibly rare occasions when he failed in spite of possessing the relevant ability. This is a third consideration supporting the idea that Q is less dispositional than P.

These considerations show that in various ways it is more absurd to maintain that *If P then R* entails Q than it is to maintain that *If Q then R* entails P. So the second stage in Austin's criticism of Nowell-Smith, when its implications are worked out in detail, evidently does go beyond the first stage. He has produced an effective *reductio ad absurdum* of one way of arguing from the thesis that P entails *If Q then R* to the converse thesis. However, if the question is whether the dispositional analysis is true, his argument is not so effective as he supposed. For, first, it only attacks the converse thesis, that *If Q then R* entails P, leaving the direct form of the thesis unscathed. Secondly, it only undermines one argument for the converse thesis, leaving it an open question whether the converse thesis is true. Thirdly, the case for saying that the converse thesis that *If Q then R* entails *P* is not true, is not nearly so strong as the case for saying that the converse thesis that *If P then R* entails *Q* is not true. So Austin's criticism of the dispositional analysis of ascriptions of abilities to people is blunted by the very thing that makes his *reductio ad absurdum* of the argument that he attributes to Nowell-Smith so effective.

VII

Austin on Locutionary and Illocutionary Acts[1]

IN ATTEMPTING to explore Austin's notion of an *illocutionary act* I have found his corresponding notion of a *locutionary act* very unhelpful and have been forced to adopt a quite different distinction between illocutionary acts and propositional acts.[2] I think this difference is more than a matter of taxonomical preference and involves important philosophical issues—issues such as the nature of statements, the way truth and falsehood relate to statements, and the way what sentences mean relates to what speakers mean when they utter sentences. In this paper I want to explain my reasons for rejecting Austin's distinction and for introducing certain other distinctions, and in so doing to show how these questions bear on some of the larger philosophical issues.

I

The main theme of Austin's *How to Do Things with Words* is the replacement of the original distinction between performatives and constatives by a general theory of speech acts. The original distinction (the 'special theory') was supposed to be a distinction between utterances which are statements or descriptions, and utterances which are acts, such as, for example, promises, apologies, bets, or warnings. It is supposed to be a distinction between

---

[1] I am grateful to Steven Davis, Dagmar Searle, and the editors of the *Philosophical Review* for comments on earlier drafts of this paper. (The paper has been previously published in the *Philosophical Review*, vol. lxxvii, no. 4 (October 1968).) It is reprinted here with the permission of the author and the *Philosophical Review*.

[2] J. R. Searle, 'What is a Speech Act?', in *Philosophy in America*, ed. Max Black (London, 1965); and J. R. Searle, *Speech Acts, An Essay in the Philosophy of Language* (Cambridge, 1969), ch. 2.

utterances which are sayings and utterances which are doings. Austin shows in detail how attempts to make the distinction precise along these lines only show that it collapses. One is tempted to say that whereas constatives can be true or false, performatives cannot be true or false, but felicitous or infelicitous, depending on whether they are performed correctly, completely, and sincerely in accord with some antecedent set of conventions. But, as Austin's careful researches show, certain performatives can be assessed as true or false (for example, warnings), and constatives can be assessed in the felicitous–infelicitous dimension as well (for example, an utterance of the sentence 'All John's children are asleep' is infelicitous if John has no children). Eventually the conclusion becomes obvious: making a statement or giving a description is just as much performing an act as making a promise or giving a warning. What was originally supposed to be a special case of utterances (performatives) swallows the general case (constatives), which now turn out to be only certain kinds of speech acts among others. Statements, descriptions, and so forth are only other classes of illocutionary acts on all fours, as illocutionary acts, with promises, commands, apologies, bets, and warnings.

So far so good. But now Austin introduces a second distinction which will replace in the general theory what was hoped to be achieved by the performative–constative distinction in the special theory, the distinction between locutionary and illocutionary acts. As initially presented, it is the distinction between uttering a sentence with a certain *meaning*, in one sense of 'meaning' which Austin characterizes as 'sense and reference' (the locutionary act) and uttering a sentence with a certain *force* (the illocutionary act). This can be illustrated by the following example. A serious literal utterance[3] by a single speaker of the sentence 'I am going to do it' can be (can have the force of) a promise, a prediction, a threat, a warning, a statement of intention, and so forth. Yet the sentence is not ambiguous; it has one and only one literal meaning. It has one sense, and different utterances of it can have the same reference. Thus different utterances of the sentence with that literal meaning, given sameness of

---

[3] I contrast 'serious' utterances with play-acting, teaching a language, reciting poems, practicing pronunciation, etc., and I contrast 'literal' with metaphorical, sarcastic, etc.

reference, can be one and only one locutionary act. They can be different locutionary tokens of one locutionary type. But those same utterances with the same sense and reference could be any of a number of different illocutionary acts; they could have different illocutionary forces, because, for example, one could be (could have the force of) a promise, while another was a prediction, yet another a threat, and so forth. Utterances which were different tokens of the same locutionary type could be tokens of different illocutionary types.

Now the first difficulty that one encounters with Austin's distinction is that it seems that it cannot be completely general, in the sense of marking off two mutually exclusive classes of acts, because, for some sentences at least, meaning, in Austin's sense, determines (at least one) illocutionary force of the utterance of the sentence. Thus, though the sentence 'I am going to do it' can be seriously uttered with its literal meaning in any number of illocutionary acts, what about the sentence 'I hereby promise that I am going to do it'? Its serious and literal utterance must be a promise.[4] It may on occasion be other illocutionary acts as well, but it must at least be a promise—that is, an illocutionary act of a certain type. The meaning of the sentence determines an illocutionary force of its utterances in such a way that serious utterances of it with that literal meaning will have that particular force. The description of the act as a happily performed locutionary act, since it involves the meaning of the sentence, is already a description of the illocutionary act, since a particular illocutionary act is determined by that meaning. They are one and the same act. Uttering the sentence with a certain meaning is, Austin tells us, performing a certain locutionary act; uttering a sentence with a certain force is performing a certain illocutionary act; but where a certain force is part of the meaning, where the meaning uniquely determines a particular force, there are not two different acts but two different labels for the same act. Austin says that each is an abstraction from the total speech act, but the difficulty is that for a large class of cases—certainly all those involving the performative use of illocutionary verbs—there is no way of abstracting the locutionary act which does not catch an illocutionary act with it.

---

[4] Assuming that the act is successful, that is, that the conditions of successful utterance are satisfied.

Abstracting the meaning of the utterance will necessarily abstract an illocutionary force wherever that force is included in that meaning.

The *concept* of an utterance with a certain meaning (that is, the concept of a locutionary act) is indeed a different concept from the *concept* of an utterance with a certain force (that is, the concept of an illocutionary act).[5] But there are many sentences whose meaning is such as to determine that the serious utterance of the sentence with its literal meaning has a particular force. Hence the *class* of illocutionary acts will contain members of the *class* of locutionary acts. The concepts are different but they denote overlapping classes. For cases such as the performative use of illocutionary verbs the attempt to *abstract* the locutionary meaning from illocutionary force would be like abstracting unmarried men from bachelors. So our first tentative conclusion—we shall have to revise it later—is that the locutionary–illocutionary distinction is not completely general, because some locutionary acts are illocutionary acts.[6]

As it stands there is an easy, but in the end unsatisfactory, way out of this difficulty. A locutionary act is defined by Austin as the uttering of certain vocables with a certain sense and reference. But if that is absolutely all there is to the definition, then, it could be argued, the objection just raised is not really valid; because even for such cases as an utterance of 'I hereby order you to leave' there is still a distinction between uttering the sentence with (that is, as having) a certain sense and reference on the one hand (the locutionary act) and actually bringing off a *successfully* performed illocutionary act. For example, I might utter the sentence to someone who does not hear me, and so I would not succeed in performing the illocutionary act of order-

---

[5] Throughout this paper I use these as equivalent. But on one possible interpretation Austin meant to distinguish illocutionary acts of type *F* from utterances with illocutionary force *F* on the grounds that an utterance may have force *F* even though the purported act is not, as a whole, successful, and hence has not strictly speaking, been performed. I grant that as a possible interpretation, but nothing in my arguments hinges on accepting my interpretation. The arguments are statable in essentially the same form on either interpretation.

[6] Austin was familiar with this difficulty. I discussed it with him in Hilary term of 1956, and he mentioned it briefly in his lectures of that term. It has also been discussed by L. J. Cohen, 'Do Illocutionary Forces Exist?', *Philosophical Quarterly*, 14 (1964), 118–37; and briefly by J. O. Urmson, 'J. L. Austin', *Encyclopedia of Philosophy*, ed. Edwards, vol. i. Cohen unfortunately seems to conclude that there are no such things as illocutionary forces. This conclusion seems unwarranted.

ing him, even though I did perform a locutionary act since I uttered the sentence with its usual meaning (in Austin's terminology in such cases I fail to secure 'illocutionary uptake'). Or to take a different example, I might not be in a position to issue orders to him, if, say, he is a general and I am a private (and so the 'order' would again be 'infelicitous' in Austin's terminology). So, one might argue, Austin's distinction between locutionary and illocutionary acts is still intact even for cases containing the performative use of illocutionary verbs. It is a distinction between the simple meaningful utterance and the successfully performed complete illocutionary act. The successfully performed illocutionary act requires all sorts of conditions not required by the locutionary act.

But this answer to my original objection is unsatisfactory for at least two reasons. First, it reduces the locutionary–illocutionary distinction to a distinction between trying and succeeding in performing an illocutionary act. Since the conditions of success for the performance of the act are—except for the general conditions on any kind of linguistic communication[7]—a function of the meaning of the sentence, then uttering that sentence seriously with its literal meaning will be at least purporting to perform an illocutionary act of giving an order. And the only distinction left for such sentences will be the distinction between that part of trying to perform an illocutionary act which consists in uttering the sentence seriously with its literal meaning, and actually succeeding in performing an illocutionary act, which is a much less interesting distinction than the original distinction between the locutionary act and the illocutionary act.[8]

But secondly, even if we adopt this way out it now leaves us with two quite different distinctions, for the distinction between this part of trying and actually succeeding is different from the original distinction between an utterance with a particular meaning and an utterance with a particular illocutionary force.

So, at this preliminary stage of our discussion, we find two

[7] In part these conditions involve what I elsewhere call input–output conditions (Searle, op. cit., ch. 3) and Austin calls conditions of illocutionary uptake (Austin, op. cit., Lecture 9).

[8] Furthermore, Austin himself repeatedly insists that the distinction between 'attempt and achievement' applies to all the kinds of acts. See for example, op. cit., p. 104.

quite different distinctions hiding under the locutionary–illocutionary cloak. One is an interesting but not completely general (in the sense of marking off two mutually exclusive classes) distinction between the meaning of an utterance and the force of the utterance, the second is a not so interesting but general distinction between a certain part of trying and succeeding in performing an illocutionary act.

II

All this, it seems to me, is still very tentative; and it is now time to probe deeper in an effort both to push the objection to the bottom and at the same time to do full justice to the subtlety of Austin's thought.

Austin analyses the locutionary act into three parts. The *phonetic act* is the act of uttering certain noises, the *phatic act* is the act of uttering certain vocables or words, and the *rhetic act* is the act of using those vocables with a more or less definite sense and reference. Taken together, these constitute the locutionary act. Each of these is an 'abstraction', as are indeed the locutionary and illocutionary acts themselves. When he contrasts locutionary and illocutionary acts, Austin gives the following as examples of the contrast.

Locution: He said to me 'Shoot her!' meaning by 'shoot' shoot and referring by 'her' to *her*.
Illocution: He urged (or advised, ordered, etc.) me to shoot her.
Locution: He said to me, 'You can't do that.'
Illocution: He protested against my doing it [pp. 101–2].

Notice that here he uses the *oratio recta* (direct quotation) form to identify locutionary acts and *oratio obliqua* (indirect quotation) to identify illocutionary acts. The sentence which identifies the locutionary act contains quotation marks, the sentence which identifies the illocutionary act does not. But on page 95, when discussing the internal structure of locutionary acts, he distinguishes within the locutionary act between the phatic act and the rhetic act, and here he identifies the phatic act by using the *oratio recta* form with quotation marks and identifies the rhetic act by using indirect quotation.

He said 'I shall be there' (phatic). He said he would be there (rhetic).

He said 'Get out' (phatic). He told me to get out (rhetic).

He said 'Is it in Oxford or Cambridge?' (phatic). He asked whether it was in Oxford or Cambridge (rhetic).

Prima facie it seems inconsistent to identify the locutionary act on one page by the use of direct quotation, contrasting it with the illocutionary act which is identified by the use of indirect quotation, and then on another page to identify the rhetic part of the locutionary act by the use of indirect quotation, contrasting it with another part of the locutionary act, the phatic act, which is identified by the use of direct quotation. But as Austin sees, it is not *necessarily* inconsistent, because since the locutionary act is defined as uttering a sentence with a certain sense and reference (meaning) then that sense and reference will determine an appropriate indirect-speech form for reporting the locutionary act. For example, if the sentence is in the imperative, the sense of the imperative mood determines that the appropriate *oratio obliqua* form will be 'He told me to' or some such; if it is in the interrogative, it will be 'He asked me whether'. Both of these are precisely examples Austin gives. But now notice a crucial difficulty with the indirect forms: the verb-phrases in the reports of *rhetic* acts invariably contain *illocutionary* verbs. They are indeed very general illocutionary verbs, but they are illocutionary none the less. Consider 'He told me to X'. Does not the form 'He told me to' cover a very general class of illocutionary forces, which includes such specific illocutionary forces as 'He ordered, commanded, requested, urged, advised, me to'? The verbs in Austin's examples of indirect-speech reports of rhetic acts are all illocutionary verbs of a very general kind, which stand in relation to the verbs in his reports of illocutionary acts as genus to species. That is, there are different species of the genus telling someone to do something—for example, ordering, requesting, commanding—but 'tell . . . to' is as much an illocutionary verb as any of these others, and a little reflection will show that it meets Austin's criteria for illocutionary verbs. In short, on close examination we discover that, in characterizing rhetic acts, Austin has inadvertently characterized them as illocutionary acts. Furthermore, there is no way to give an indirect-speech report of a rhetic act (performed in the utterance of a complete sentence) which does not turn the report into the report of an illocutionary act. Why is that?

We saw above that the original locutionary–illocutionary distinction is best designed to account for those cases where the meaning of the sentence is, so to speak, force-neutral—that is, where its literal utterance did not serve to distinguish a particular illocutionary force. But now further consideration will force us to the following conclusion: no sentence is completely force-neutral. Every sentence has some illocutionary force-potential, if only of a very broad kind, built into its meaning. For example, even the most primitive of the old-fashioned grammatical categories of indicative, interrogative, and imperative sentences already contain determinants of illocutionary force. For this reason there is no specification of a locutionary act performed in the utterance of a complete sentence which will not determine the specification of an illocutionary act. Or, to put it more bluntly, on the characterization that Austin has so far given us of locutionary as opposed to illocutionary acts, there are (in the utterance of complete sentences) no rhetic acts as opposed to illocutionary acts at all. There are indeed phonetic acts of uttering certain noises, phatic acts of uttering certain vocables or words (and sentences), and illocutionary acts such as making statements, asking questions, giving commands, but it does not seem that there are or can be acts of using those vocables in sentences with sense and reference which are not already (at least purported) illocutionary acts.

Austin might seem to be granting this when he says that to perform a locutionary act is in general and *eo ipso* to perform an illocutionary act (p. 98). But his point here is that each is only a separate *abstraction* from the total speech act. He still thinks that locutionary and illocutionary acts are separate and mutually exclusive abstractions. The point I am making now is that there is no way to abstract a rhetic act in the utterance of a complete sentence which does not abstract an illocutionary act as well, for a rhetic[9] act is always an illocutionary act of one kind or another.

In Section I we tentatively concluded that *some* members of the class of locutionary acts were members of the class of illocutionary acts. It now emerges that *all* the members of the class of

[9] It has to be emphasized that we are considering here (and throughout) utterances of whole sentences. If we confine ourselves to certain parts of sentences we shall be able to make a distinction. More of this in Sec. IV, pp. 155–9.

locutionary acts (performed in the utterance of complete sentences) are members of the class of illocutionary acts, because every rhetic act, and hence every locutionary act, is an illocutionary act. The concepts *locutionary* act and *illocutionary* act are indeed different, just as the concepts *terrier* and *dog* are different. But the conceptual difference is not sufficient to establish a distinction between separate classes of acts, because just as every terrier is a dog, so every locutionary act is an illocutionary act. Since a rhetic act involves the utterance of a sentence with a certain meaning and the sentence invariably as part of its meaning contains some indicator of illocutionary force, no utterance of a sentence with its meaning is completely force-neutral. Every serious literal utterance contains some indicators of force as part of meaning, which is to say that every rhetic act is an illocutionary act.

So if the distinction is construed, as I think it must be, as between mutually exclusive classes of acts, however abstract they may be, it collapses. There is still left a distinction between the literal meaning of a sentence and the intended force of its utterance (as illustrated by the example 'I am going to do it'), but that is only a special case of the distinction between literal meaning and intended meaning, between what the sentence means and what the speaker means in its utterance, and it has no special relevance to the general theory of illocutionary forces, because intended illocutionary force is only one of the aspects (sense and reference are others) in which intended speaker-meaning may go beyond literal sentence-meaning.

Austin sometimes talks as if in addition to the meaning of sentences there were a further set of conventions of illocutionary force; but in precisely those cases where there is a distinction between force and meaning, the force is not carried by a convention but by other features of the context, including the intentions of the speaker; and as soon as force is tied down by an explicit convention it becomes, or in general tends to become, part of meaning. For example, we have a convention that 'How do you do?' is a greeting used when being introduced and not a question, but then that is part of the meaning of this idiom. Someone who thinks that this sentence is paraphrasable as 'In what manner or condition do you perform?' or who takes it as permutable into such questions as 'How does he do?' or 'How do I do?' has not understood the meaning of this (contemporary English) idiom.

Where does that leave us now? Austin's original taxonomy included the following kinds of acts:

Locutionary   phonetic
                phatic
                rhetic

Illocutionary

What we really argued is that the rhetic act as originally characterized has to be eliminated and, with it, the locutionary act as originally characterized. So we are left with the following:

Phonetic
Phatic
Illocutionary

For any of these we can distinguish between trying and succeeding, so *that* distinction will not resurrect any special distinction between locutionary and illocutionary acts; and furthermore there is an additional distinction between what a speaker means by the utterance of a sentence and what that sentence means literally, but that distinction will not preserve a *general* distinction between locutionary meaning and illocutionary force, since the locutionary meaning of sentences always contains some illocutionary force-potential, and hence the locutionary meaning of utterances determines (at least some) illocutionary force of utterances.

III

Underlying the objections I have been making to Austin's account are certain linguistic principles, which it seems to me will enable us to offer a diagnosis of what I am claiming are the limitations in that account. I shall state them baldly and then try to explain what they mean and what relevance they have to the present discussion.

1. Whatever can be meant can be said. I call this the Principle of Expressibility.

2. The meaning of a sentence is determined by the meanings of all its meaningful components.

3. The illocutionary forces of utterances may be more or less

specific; and there are several different principles of distinction for distinguishing different types of illocutionary acts.

1. Often we mean more than we actually *say*. You ask me, 'Are you going to the party?' I say, 'Yes'. But what I mean is 'Yes, I am going to the party', not 'Yes, it is a fine day'. Similarly, I might say, 'I'll come', and mean it as a promise— that is, mean it as I would mean 'I hereby promise I will come', if I were uttering that sentence seriously and meaning literally what I said. Often I am unable to say exactly what I mean, even if I want to, because I do not know the words (if I am speaking French, say) or, worse yet, because there are no words or other linguistic devices for saying what I mean. But even in cases where I am unable to say exactly what I mean it is in principle possible to come to be able to say what I mean. I can, in principle if not in fact, always enrich my knowledge of the language I am speaking; or, more radically, if the language is not rich enough, if it simply lacks the resources for saying what I mean, I can, in principle at least, enrich the language. The general point, however, is that whatever one can mean one can, in principle if not in fact, say or come to be able to say. The lexical and syntactical resources of languages are indeed finite. But there are no limits in principle to their enrichment. I think this is an important principle, but I am not going to develop all of its consequences here.

2. The principle that the meaning of a sentence is entirely determined by the meanings of its meaningful parts I take as obviously true; what is not so obviously true, however, is that these include more than words (or morphemes) and surface word-order. The meaningful components of a sentence include also its deep syntactic structure and the stress and intonation contour of its utterance. Words and word-order are not the only elements which determine meaning.

3. The illocutionary forces of utterances may be more or less indeterminate. Suppose I ask you to do something for me. My utterance may be, for example, a request or an entreaty or a plea. Yet the description 'I asked you to do it' is, though less specific than any of these, none the less a correct description. Furthermore, I may not at all know myself which of the specific possibilities I meant it as. My own intentions may have been indeterminate within this range (which is not to say that they

can be completely indeterminate—that I may not know if it was a statement, an order, or a question). There are really two separate points here. One is that *descriptions* of illocutionary acts may be more or less determinate. The second and more important, which I now wish to emphasize, is that the acts themselves may be more or less definite and precise as to their illocutionary force.

One might think of illocutionary acts (and hence illocutionary verbs) as on a continuum of determinateness or specificity, but even this would not do full justice to the complexity of the situation, for under the rubric 'illocutionary forces' are all sorts of different principles of distinction. Here, by way of example, are four different principles of distinction: the point or purpose of the act (for example, the difference between a question and a statement), the relative status of the speaker and hearer (for example, the difference between a command and a request), the degree of commitment undertaken (for example, the difference between an expression of intent and a promise), the conversational placing and role of the act (for example, the difference between a reply to what someone has said and an objection to what he has said).

Now how does all this relate to Austin's distinctions? Consider point 3 first. Austin was much impressed by the surface-structure of natural languages, particularly English. The fact that he could get a list of 'the third power of ten' illocutionary verbs was important to his conception of illocutionary acts. But there is nothing mutually *exclusive* about all the members of the list nor is the total list necessarily *exhaustive*. The same utterance may be correctly described by any number of different illocutionary verbs on the list, or the act may have been so special and precise in its intent that none of the existing words can quite characterize it exactly. If we think of illocutionary forces as existing on a continuum or continua of specificity (point 3), then the fact that our existing English verbs stop at certain points and not others on some continuum is a more or less contingent fact about English. It so happens that we have the word 'promise', but we might not have had it. We might have had ten different words for different kinds of promises, or indeed we might instead have had only one word to cover our present classes of promises, vows, and pledges.

A neglect of point 3, then, seems one possible explanation of why Austin did not see that the supposedly locutionary verb phrases 'tell someone to do something', 'say that', 'ask whether' are as much illocutionary verb phrases as 'state that', 'order someone to', or 'promise someone that'. They are indeed more general, but that makes their relation to the more specific verbs that of genus term to species term or determinable term to determinate term. It does not, as Austin seems to suggest (on p. 95),[10] make their denotation a different type of act altogether.

Now let us consider point 1. A commonplace of recent philosophizing about language has been the distinction between sentences and the speech acts performed in the utterances of those sentences. Valuable as this distinction is, there has also been a tendency to overemphasize it to the extent of neglecting the Principle of Expressibility. There is indeed a category distinction between the sentence and the illocutionary act performed in its utterance, but the illocutionary act or acts which can be performed in the utterance of a sentence are a function of the meaning of the sentence. And, more importantly, according to the Principle, foe every illocutionary act one intends to perform, it is possible to utter a sentence the literal meaning of which is such as to determine that its serious literal utterance in an appropriate context will be a performance of that act. Austin's distinction between locutionary and illocutionary acts is supposed to be a distinction between uttering a sentence with a certain meaning, in the sense of sense and reference, and uttering it with a certain force; but according to the Principle, whenever one wishes to make an utterance with force F, it is always possible to utter a sentence the meaning of which expresses exactly force F, since if it is possible to mean (intend) that force it is possible to say that force literally. Often, of course, as I have noted, and as Austin emphasizes, the said-meaning and the meant-force come apart, but this is, though quite common, a contingent fact about the way we speak and not a conceptual truth about the concept of illocutionary force.

A neglect of the Principle of Expressibility (point 1) seems to be one of the reasons why Austin overestimated the distinction between meaning and force. It is a consequence of the Principle,

---

[10] In fact 'ask' crops up on p. 161 as well, as an example of an 'expositive' illocutionary verb.

together with the point that every sentence contains some deter-
miners of illocutionary force, that the study of the meanings of
sentences and the study of the illocutionary acts which could be
performed in the utterances of sentences are not two different
studies, but one and the same study from two different points
of view. This is so because, to repeat, for every possible illocutionary act a speaker may wish to perform there is a possible
sentence (or sequence of sentences) the serious literal utterance
of which under appropriate circumstances would be a performance of that illocutionary act, and for every sentence some
illocutionary force-potential is included in the meaning of the
sentence. So there could not, according to my analysis, be a
general and mutually exclusive distinction between the meaning
and the force of literal utterances, both because the force which
the speaker intends can in principle always be given an exact
expression in a sentence with a particular meaning, and because
the meaning of every sentence already contains some deter-
miners of illocutionary force.

A neglect of point 2 is also involved in our diagnosis. Austin
characterized the rhetic act in terms of uttering a sentence with
a certain sense and reference. The difficulty, however, with this
characterization is that the *terminology* of sense and reference
inclines us to focus on words, or at most phrases, as the bearers of
sense and reference. But of course deep syntactic structure, stress,
and intonation-contour are bearers of meaning as well, as we
noted in point 2. One of the possible reasons why Austin
neglected the extent to which force was part of meaning is that
his use of the Fregean terminology of sense and reference shifted
the focus of emphasis away from some of the most common
elements in the meaning of a sentence which determine the
illocutionary force-potential of the sentence: deep syntactic
structure, stress, intonation-contour (and, in written speech,
punctuation). If one thinks of sentential meaning as a matter of
sense and reference, and tacitly takes sense and reference as
properties of words and phrases, then one is likely to neglect
those elements of meaning which are not matters of words and
phrases, and it is often precisely those elements which in virtue
of their meaning are such crucial determinants of illocutionary
force.

IV

Though I do not think Austin was completely successful in characterizing a locutionary–illocutionary distinction, there are certain real distinctions which underlie his effort. The first I mentioned is a distinction between that part of trying which consists solely in making a serious literal utterance and actually succeeding in performing an illocutionary act. The second is the distinction between what a sentence means and what the speaker may mean in uttering it, with the special case of serious literal utterance where the meaning of the sentence uttered does not completely exhaust the illocutionary intentions of the speaker in making the utterance. Now I wish to consider a third distinction which I think Austin had in mind.

He says (pp. 144–5):

> With the constative utterance, we abstract from the illocutionary (let alone the perlocutionary) aspects of the speech act, and we concentrate on the locutionary . . . With the performative utterance, we attend as much as possible to the illocutionary force of the utterance, and abstract from the dimension of correspondence with facts.

These and other remarks suggest to me that Austin may have had in mind the distinction between the content or, as some philosophers call it, the proposition, in an illocutionary act and the force or illocutionary type of the act.[11] Thus, for example, the proposition that I will leave may be a common content of different utterances with different illocutionary forces, for I can threaten, warn, state, predict, or promise that I will leave. We need to distinguish in the total illocutionary act the type of act from the content of the act. This distinction, in various forms, is by now common in philosophy and can be found in philosophers as diverse as Frege, Hare, Lewis, and Meinong. If we wish to present this distinction in speech act terms (within a general theory of speech acts) a taxonomically promising way of doing it might be the following. We need to distinguish the illocutionary act from the propositional act—that is, the act of *expressing the proposition* (a phrase which is neutral as to illocutionary force). And the point of the distinction is that the identity

---

[11] Austin once told me he thought a distinction could be made along these lines—but it is not clear that he intended the locutionary–illocutionary distinction to capture it.

conditions of the propositional act are not the same as the identity conditions of the total illocutionary act, since the same propositional act can occur in all sorts of different illocutionary acts. When we are concerned with so-called constatives we do indeed tend to concentrate on the propositional aspect rather than the illocutionary force, for it is the proposition which involves 'correspondence with the facts'. When we consider so-called performatives we attend as much as possible to the illocutionary force of the utterance (for example, 'I know you *said* you'd come, but do you *promise*?').

Symbolically, we might represent the sentence as containing an illocutionary force-indicating device and a propositional content indicator. Thus:

$$F(p),$$

where the range of possible values for F will determine the range of illocutionary forces, and the p is a variable over the infinite range of possible propositions.[12] Notice that in this form the distinction is not subject to the objections we made to the original locutionary–illocutionary distinction. The propositional act is not represented, either in the symbolism or in natural languages, by the entire sentence, but only by those portions of the sentence which do not include the indicators of illocutionary force. Thus the propositional act is a genuine abstraction from the total illocutionary act, and—so construed—no propositional act is by itself an illocutionary act.

I do not know that this is one of the things Austin had in mind with the locutionary–illocutionary distinction, but the remarks quoted above suggest to me that it is (especially in connection with certain other remarks, such as his including 'refer' among locutionary verbs; in my terminology referring is characteristically part of the propositional act, and referring expressions are portions of sentences, not whole sentences). But whether or not Austin ever intended this, it seems to me to be useful in its own right and to be one of the distinctions we need with which to supplant the original locutionary–illocutionary distinction.[13]

---

[12] Not all illocutionary acts would fit this model. For example, 'Hurrah for Manchester United' or 'Down with Caesar' would be of the form $F(n)$, where n is replaceable by referring expressions.

[13] It is also a distinction I employ elsewhere (see references cited in footnote 2).

So far I have said that there are at least three different distinctions[14] which can be extracted from the locutionary–illocutionary distinction:

(1) The distinction between a certain aspect of trying and succeeding in performing an illocutionary act.

(2) The distinction between the literal meaning of the sentence and what the speaker means (by way of illocutionary force) when he utters it.

(3) The distinction between propositional acts and illocutionary acts.

I now want to use this last distinction in an examination of one of Austin's most important discoveries, the discovery that constatives are illocutionary acts as well as performatives, or, in short, the discovery that statements are speech acts.

The difficulty with this thesis as Austin presents it in *How to Do Things with Words* is that the word 'statement' is structurally ambiguous. Like many nominalized verb-forms it has what traditional grammarians call the act–object, or sometimes the process–product, ambiguity. A modern transformational grammarian would say that it is structurally ambiguous as it has at least two different derivations from (phrase-markers containing) the verb 'state'. 'Statement' can mean either the *act of stating* or *what is stated*. (Possibly it has other meanings as well, but these are the most important for present purposes.) Here are two sentences in which these two meanings of 'statement' are quite clearly distinct.

1. The statement of our position took all of the morning session.

2. The statement that all men are mortal is true.

Notice that you cannot say 'The statement that all men are mortal took ten seconds.' But you can say:

3. The statement of the statement that all men are mortal took ten seconds.

This just means that it took ten seconds to *make* the statement, or

---

[14] There is a fourth distinction, which I do not discuss here, between the illocutionary act performed by the speaker and what he implies in performing it. Cf. H. P. Grice, 'The Causal Theory of Perception' (secs. 2–4), *Proceedings of the Aristotelian Society*, supp. vol. (1961); and J. R. Searle, 'Assertions and Aberrations', *British Analytical Philosophy*, edd. B. A. O. Williams and A. C. Montefiore (London 1966), for some preliminary discussion of this distinction.

that the act of stating took ten seconds. Let us call these two senses the statement-act sense and the statement-object sense. Austin's discovery that statements are illocutionary acts holds for the act sense, but not for the object sense.

But that is not necessarily a weakness since the same distinction can be made for a great many other nominalized forms of the illocutionary verbs. The real significance of Austin's discovery is that 'state' is an illocutionary verb like any other, and this leads us to the further observation that its nominalized forms share features with nominalized forms of illocutionary verbs; in particular in the '-ment' form 'state' shares the act–object ambiguity. (As Austin might have said, it's the verb which wears the trousers.)[15]

The failure to take into account the structural ambiguity of 'statement', however, had very important consequences for certain other parts of Austin's theory of language. For since statements are speech acts, and since statements can be true or false, it appears that that which is true or false is a speech act. But this inference is fallacious, as it involves a fallacy of ambiguity. Statement-acts are speech acts, and statement-objects (as well as propositions) are what can be true or false. And the view that it is the act of stating which is true or false is one of the most serious weaknesses of Austin's theory of truth.[16]

Confining ourselves to 'constatives', the distinction between statement-acts and statement-objects can be explained in terms of our distinction between propositional content and illocutionary force as follows:

The statement-act   = the act of stating.
                     = the act of stating a proposition.
                     = the act of expressing a proposition with a constative (I would prefer to call it 'statemental') illocutionary force.
                     = the act of making a statement-object.

[15] To complicate matters further, not all literal utterances of 'state' are connected with what philosophers call 'statements' at all. Consider 'State the question again, please' or 'He restated his promise'. Neither of these is a 'constative'.

[16] As Strawson pointed out in the 'Truth' symposium, *Proceedings of the Aristotelian Society*, supp. vol. (1950).

The statement-object = what is stated (construed as stated).

= the proposition (construed as stated).

Propositions but not acts can be true or false; thus statement-objects but not statement-acts can be true or false. In the characterization of statement-object we have to add the phrase 'construed as stated' because of course what is stated, the proposition, can also be the content of a question, of a promise, the antecedent of a hypothetical, and so forth. It is neutral as to the illocutionary force with which it is expressed, but statements are not neutral as to illocutionary force, so 'statement' in its object sense is not synonymous with 'proposition', but only with 'proposition construed as stated'.

So, to conclude this point, the distinction between the propositional act and the illocutionary act and the corresponding distinction between propositions and illocutions enables us to account for certain traditional problems in the notion of a statement. Statement-acts are illocutionary acts of stating. Statement-objects are propositions (contrued as stated). The latter but not the former can be true or false. And it is the confusion between these which prevented Austin from seeing both that statements can be speech-acts and that statements can be true or false, though acts cannot have truth-values.

What is the outcome of our discussion of locutionary and illocutionary speech acts? We are left with:

Phonetic acts
Phatic acts
Propositional acts
Illocutionary acts

Propositional acts are all that we can salvage from the original conception of a rhetic act, in so far as we wish to distinguish rhetic acts from illocutionary acts. But whether or not Austin had them in mind, they are independently motivated and not subject to the objections we made to Austin's account of locutionary acts.

VIII

Locutionary and Illocutionary Acts

L. W. FORGUSON

I FIND myself in considerable sympathy with the more constructive aspects of Professor Searle's paper. In particular, his attempt to make use of the notion of a proposition in the analysis of speech acts is very attractive. I cannot, however, agree with his destructive theses, which aim to undermine Austin's fundamental distinction between locutionary and illocutionary acts. His arguments to this end arise, I think, out of a fundamental misunderstanding of Austin's views. In this paper I intend to investigate Austin's notion of a locutionary act, in the hope of showing that the notion is more hospitable than Professor Searle has allowed, to examine in somewhat less detail the connections Austin saw between locutionary and illocutionary acts, and to use the results of these investigations to show how Professor Searle's short way with the distinction between locutionary and illocutionary acts goes astray.

I

The first seven sections of *How to Do Things with Words* chronicle the rise and fall of the performative–constative distinction. The failure to find a criterion which will effectively distinguish performatives from all other sorts of utterance, and the resulting discovery that every utterance has a 'performative' dimension, led Austin to reconsider, 'from the ground up', the many different ways in which saying something is doing something, the many ways in which the issuing of an utterance is the performance of an act. He first considers:

a whole group of senses . . . in which to say anything must always be to do something, the group of senses which together add up to 'saying' something, in the full sense of 'say'. We may agree . . . that to say anything is

> always to perform the act of uttering certain noises (a 'phonetic' act), and the utterance is a phone;

> always to perform the act of uttering certain vocables or words, i.e. noises of certain types belonging to *and as* belonging to a certain vocabulary, in a certain construction, i.e. conforming to and as conforming to a certain grammar, with a certain intonation, etc. This act we may call a 'phatic' act, and the utterance of which it is the act of uttering a 'pheme';

> generally to perform the act of using that pheme or its constituents with a certain more or less definite 'sense' and a more or less definite 'reference' (which together are equivalent to 'meaning'). This act we may call a 'rhetic' act, and the utterance which it is the act of uttering a 'rheme' (pp. 92–3).

Each of these ancillary acts is present in any fully 'happy' utterance. Taken together, they constitute the *locutionary* act: the act of saying something, or the act of saying what one says. The locutionary act is in turn contrasted with the *illocutionary* act—an act, such as betting, requesting, or promising—which is performed *in* saying what one says, and with the *perlocutionary* act—an act, such as convincing, persuading, or frightening—which is accomplished as a result or consequence of saying what one says. All of these acts are themselves said to be 'abstractions' from the *total* speech act—the ultimate object of study—for which, curiously enough, Austin provides no technical label.

I now want to examine the constitution of the locutionary act in more detail, in order to elucidate its nature *vis-à-vis* the ancillary acts which are its components, and to clarify the relationships Austin intended it to have] to the illocutionary act.

The phonetic act is 'the act of uttering certain noises'. At this level of abstraction, any noises will do. They need not be phonemes of any language, though if the act is to be anything more than merely a phonetic act the noises must be phonemes; for whenever anyone performs an act of saying something 'in the full normal sense' he also performs a phonetic act *en passant*.

In order to cross the border between the phonetic and the

phatic act it is necessary to bring into consideration both the speaker's intentions and (what for lack of a better word may be called) conventions. The conventions in question are those which constitute the vocabulary and grammar of a language. Let them be called *L-conventions*. The intentions are the speaker's intentions to produce noises which conform to these *L*-conventions in a certain way: his intention to produce a series of noises which *counts as* a sentence of the language. Let us call any such intention an *L-intention*. No series of produced noises can itself be a pheme; for even if the series satisfies the relevant *L*-conventions, the requisite *L*-intentions have not been brought into the picture.

We may say, then, that a certain phonetic act constitutes a certain phatic act if and only if (*a*) the speaker intends to produce a series of noises conforming to certain linguistic conventions, and (*b*) the series of noises he produces actually does so conform, to a certain minimum degree.[1]

An investigation of the relationship between phatic and rhetic acts will involve a further clarification of the phatic act, as well as an elucidation of the nature of rhetic acts. It is hardly surprising that Professor Searle finds difficulties in this part of Austin's doctrine, in view of the fact that the concept of meaning is introduced at this stage of his analysis, and Austin does little to clarify his rather cavalier treatment of this notoriously opaque concept. Yet it is possible to characterize the relationship between phatic and rhetic acts in a way that brings out the features distinctive of each act, and which avoids potential difficulties.

A particular phonetic act constitutes a particular phatic act just in case the phone conforms to a certain set of linguistic conventions and is intended so to conform. If these conditions are satisfied, the resulting pheme is 'a unit of *language*; its typical fault is to be nonsense—meaningless' (p. 98). But to perform a rhetic act, according to Austin, is 'to use the pheme or its constituents with a certain more or less definite "sense" and a more or less definite "reference" (which together are equivalent to

---

[1] The qualification 'to a certain minimum degree' is necessitated by the realization that an utterance may fail to conform fully to the relevant *L*-conventions and still—perhaps just barely—pass muster as a phatic act. For example, a neighbour of mine, a recent German immigrant, knocks on my door and announces: 'The around the corner living man is here.' In cases of this sort, of course, there are limits, not easily specifiable in advance, beyond which deviation will effect a total phatic misfire, no matter how honourable the speaker's intentions may be.

meaning)' (p. 93). The problem here is to explain how meaning can enter the picture at both the phatic and the rhetic stages.

Suppose someone to say: 'He met her at the bank.' The speaker produces certain noises which conform to, and are intended to conform to, certain *L*-conventions: he has uttered a pheme which, since it does conform to the *L*-conventions of English, is meaningful. But his utterance is meaningful, at the phatic level of analysis, in a *determinable*, as opposed to a *determinate* sense. The distinction I have drawn between determinable and determinate meaning needs clarification.

Every pheme has a certain horizon of 'rhetic act-potential'. This horizon is determined by the syntactic, semantic, and phonological character of the pheme. That is to say, the horizon is constituted by the different possible referents to which the referring expression or expressions in the pheme may be used to refer, and by the different senses the other meaningful components in the pheme may have; and these are restricted by the phonological character of the phone which is the vehicle of the phatic act.[2] For instance, in the pheme under consideration, the horizon is constituted by, among other features, the different possible referents of 'he' and 'her',[3] of the different senses (if more than one) of 'at', 'met', 'the bank', and (given a sense of 'bank') by the different possible referents of 'the bank'. To talk about this utterance as a pheme is to talk about it in a way which leaves this horizon undetermined, given the limits imposed upon possible determinations by the *L*-conventions relevant to the constituents of the pheme.

To consider 'He met her at the bank', then, as a pheme is to consider it as an uttered sentence, but only from the point of view of a sentence-type. The following, for example, might both be determinations yielding different tokens of the same type: (*a*) 'he' refers to John Smith, 'her' refers to Margaret Jones,

---

[2] This analysis is much too simple, though it will suffice for present purposes. For one thing, the grammar of the pheme is important in this respect. 'He went outside and put on his shirt' has a different horizon from 'He put on his shirt and went outside', to cite just one example. But the horizon is actually a function not merely of words and surface grammar, but ultimately of the deep grammatical structure of the sentence. The determinable meaning of a pheme might thus be looked upon as the disjunction of the possible determinate 'readings' of the sentence involved.

[3] The number of possible referents here is infinite. But in particular cases the context will restrict the relevant possibilities.

'met' denotes yesterday afternoon, 'the bank' refers to the High Street, Oxford, office of the District Bank; (*b*) 'he' refers to Frank Brown, 'her' refers to Priscilla Pringle, 'met' denotes the first Monday of last April, 'the bank' refers to the bank of the Isis. The horizon of rhetic act-potential of this pheme is obviously quite 'broad', the only limits being that 'he' must refer to a male, etc. By contrast, the horizon of the pheme 'I, John Smith, promise to meet you, Frank Brown, in front of the High Street, Oxford, office of the District Bank tomorrow, 27 October 1968, at 2.00 p.m.' is considerably 'narrower'. In some cases (such as, perhaps, the one just mentioned) the pheme may determine rhetic act-potential to the extent that there may be only one rhetic act possible, given the character of the pheme.

In order to turn the phatic act into a rhetic act, we need only specify the female the speaker intends to refer to by his use of 'her', to specify what he intends by his use of 'bank', and so on. Where the pheme has meaning in the determinable sense, the rheme has meaning in the determinate sense. To specify what the utterance means in the determinate sense involves, as we have seen, a specification of the speaker's intentions with respect to sense and reference, which intentions function within the limits set by the conventions of the language. The rhetic act, therefore, *disambiguates* the meaning of the pheme. In cases in which the pheme completely determines rhetic act-potential, such as in one of the examples mentioned above, the disambiguation will of course be vacuous.[4]

This way of understanding the relationship between phatic and rhetic acts is, I think, implicit in Austin's talk of *using* the pheme or its constituents with a more or less definite sense and reference. And the determinate sense of meaning seems to be what he has in mind when he says that sense and reference, as characterized by him, are 'equivalent to meaning'. As Austin indicates, (p. 97), we could further subdivide the rhetic act into the subsidiary acts of naming and referring, which together 'give' sense and reference.[5] These acts are obviously constituted,

---

[4] In principle, every pheme could be absolutely unambiguous. (Searle's discussion of the 'Principle of Expressibility' in Section III of his paper makes this clear.) But in actual speech situations this is seldom the case.

[5] Following Searle, 'What is a Speech Act?' in Max Black (ed.), *Philosophy in America*, we could also include here an act of *predication*: when I say 'He met her at the bank', I refer to someone by 'he', and predicate *meeting her at the bank* of him.

within the limitations determined by the pheme, by the speaker's intentions. Let us call these intentions which disambiguate sense and reference *SR-intentions*. In view of the foregoing discussion, Austin's characterization of the rhetic act may be reformulated as follows: a certain phatic act constitutes a certain rhetic act if and only if the speaker has certain more or less definite *SR*-intentions, functioning within the horizon constituted by the pheme.

In any case of rhetic ambiguity, the appropriate questions to ask are questions about the speaker's *SR*-intentions: questions such as 'What did he mean by ". . ."?' or 'To what did he intend to refer by his use of ". . ."?' On the contrary, questions such as 'What does ". . ." mean?' or 'What does ". . ." refer to?' (i.e. to what sorts of things can ". . ." be used to refer?) are not appropriate at this stage of inquiry. For they are either questions directed to the constituents of the pheme or questions which have a bearing on the suspicion that the *L*-conventions do not countenance the possibility of using that pheme (or certain of its constituents) to fulfil the *SR*-intentions the speaker in fact had.

It is clear, however, if the foregoing discussion is correct, that part at least of what we have in mind when we talk about meaning has its home in this aspect of the total speech act. One ancillary act we always perform when we say something ('in the full normal sense') is to mean (intend) something, with regard to sense and reference, by the words that we utter. And this is represented in Austin's taxonomy, somewhat obscurely, by the difference between what the uttered sentence means (in the determinable sense)—namely, the pheme—and what the speaker means by his words (in the determinate sense): the rheme.

According to Austin, all of these ancillary acts are merely abstractions from the locutionary act, which is itself an abstraction from the total speech act. However, though they are merely abstractions from the fully happy, felicitous speech act, in 'breakdown' situations what is normally an abstraction may exist as an act in its own right to be ascribed to the speaker.[6] If

(I do not mean to suggest that Searle himself includes this act within the rhetic act.) I will return to this point later.

[6] Austin attached considerable importance to the study of 'breakdowns', for he thought that by examining cases in which things go awry with, say, human actions we may be provided with an insight into features of acts which are

the speaker does not, for instance, produce (or at any rate, if he does not intentionally produce) a sequence of sounds conforming to the conventions of some language, he fails to perform a phatic act, and hence fails to perform a rhetic act. But he has at least performed a phonetic act: phones can have an 'independent existence' of their own. Again, if the speaker performs a phatic act, but something goes wrong at the level of sense and reference, such that it is impossible to determine what the intended sense and/or reference of his utterance is, then he has not performed a rhetic act, or at least we (his audience) are at a loss to determine *what* rhetic act he has performed. But he has at any rate performed a phatic act. Rhetic acts, however, can have no 'independent existence'. For success at the rhetic stage guarantees a successful locutionary act: a locutionary act being nothing more than an act constituted by a phonetic act, plus a phatic act, plus a rhetic act. And since, as a function of the constitutive conditions of each act, a rhetic act includes a phatic act, which in turn includes a phonetic act, there can be no slip 'twixt the rhetic act and the locutionary act. Consequently, the rhetic act is a *pure* abstraction in a way the other two ancillary acts are not.

A locutionary act is an act of saying something 'in the full normal sense of "say"', and Austin's account of the locutionary act is intended to be an explanation of the full normal sense of 'say'. But it is necessary to distinguish between what someone actually says on a given occasion and any illocutionary act, such as requesting or ordering, which he performs in saying what he says.[7] It would be desirable, in this connection, to provide a list of the constitutive rules or conditions for the performance of an illocutionary act. But this is a large and difficult task, which would take us much too far afield.[8] It is, however, possible to

overlooked in cases in which everything functions smoothly. Since speech acts are acts, we should expect this method to pay dividends in the present study as well: 'In general the illocutionary act as much as the locutionary act is an abstraction only: every genuine speech-act is both. (This is similar to the way in which the phatic act, the rhetic act, etc. are mere abstractions.) But, of course, typically we distinguish different abstracted "acts" by means of the possible slips between cup and lip, that is, in this case, the different types of nonsense which may be engendered in performing them' (p. 146).

[7] As Searle remarks, it is also necessary to distinguish the illocutionary act from what a speaker implies, suggests, insinuates, etc. by what he says, or by saying what he says.

[8] Significant attempts in this direction have been made by P. F. Strawson, 'Intention and Convention in Speech Acts', *Philosophical Review* (October 1964),

provide a partial list, which will be enough to draw the general distinction Austin thought to hold between the two types of speech act.

(1) The first condition is plain enough. In order to perform an illocutionary act the speaker must perform a locutionary act. An illocutionary act is performed via the performance of a locutionary act. But what other conditions must be satisfied? Austin provides the following clues.

(2) Austin distinguishes between the *meaning* of a locutionary act and the *force* of an illocutionary act. In his initial presentation of the notion of an illocutionary act, Austin concentrates on examples in which the meaning of an utterance (in the determinate sense of sense and reference) is taken to be clear and unambiguous, but what he calls the force of the utterance is not clear and unambiguous. The best example of what he has in mind by this contrast is the first example he presents (p. 100). Someone may say 'It's going to charge' in such a context or in such a manner that, although it is clear what the speaker is saying (what he means, in terms of sense and reference, *by* 'It's going to charge'), it is not clear whether he means it *as* a warning or merely as a factual prediction. Now, to mean an utterance *as* a warning, it seems clear, is to *intend it to be* a warning, to intend that it *count* as a warning. This intention may be frustrated, of course, in any number of ways. But one thing seems clear enough: a necessary condition for an utterance's having a certain force is that the speaker intend it to have that force;[9] and this intention is to be distinguished from his *L*-intention that the noises he produces count as an utterance of the sentence 'It's about to charge'. Is this intention also to be distinguished from the speaker's *SR*-intention? Well, in this case, and cases like it,

and by Professor Searle, 'What is a Speech Act?', loc. cit. Both of these papers exploit the connection between a speaker's intentions and the concept of *non-naturally meaning something by an utterance* set forth by H. P. Grice in 'Meaning', *Philosophical Review* (July 1957). For recent developments in Grice's views on this subject, see 'Utterer's Meaning, Sentence-Meaning and Word-Meaning', *Foundations of Language* (August 1968).

[9] Austin mentions only one case in which one can be said to have performed an illocutionary act without intending to: the case in which someone absent-mindedly says 'redouble' during a bridge match where play is strict. But this case, and others like it which may be imagined, is parasitic upon the *general* feature, which is constitutive of the concept of an illocutionary act, that force is intention-dependent.

it would seem that it must be. For we have specified his *SR*-intention in saying that what he meant by 'It's about to charge' is that some particular bull, say, is in fact about to charge. But that does not tell us whether, in saying what he said, he intended to warn anyone. However, he might have said: 'I warn you that it's about to charge.' That is, he might have made his intention that his utterance be, or count as, a warning explicit, by including a word or phrase in the utterance itself the meaning of which is tied to the expression of just this intention. Furthermore, it seems to be a general feature of illocutionary acts that one could always make one's intention with respect to force explicit in just this way, though of course often one in fact does not do so. Austin indicates that he is aware of this feature of illocutionary acts when he says (p. 130) that all of the verbs he has classified as names of illocutionary acts can be used in explicit performatives (i.e. in utterances of the form 'I (verb) that (to) . . .').[10] Now this in no way counts against the claim that it is a necessary condition for the performance of an illocutionary act that the speaker intend his utterance to have a certain force. But it does show that sometimes this intention is imbedded in the speaker's *SR*-intention: sometimes what he intends with respect to force is included in, and carried by, what he intends (in the determinate sense) with respect to meaning.

At this point one might want to insist that even in those cases in which the utterance itself doesn't contain a word or phrase (or some other linguistic device, such as special stress, etc.) which serves to make the speaker's intention with respect to force explicit, no extra 'force-intention' is required; for even in these cases the speaker's intention with respect to force is included within his *SR*-intention. The intention, or this part of it, is simply not made explicit. Thus, under this interpretation, to say that by 'It's going to charge' the speaker means that some particular bull is in fact about to charge just does not *fully* specify what he means by his utterance. I see no *a priori* objection to adopting this interpretation, for both interpretations preserve the underlying distinction: namely, sometimes the

---

[10] He does say, however, that the fact that we cannot in general use verbs which are names of perlocutionary acts in explicit performatives is 'at best very slippery' as a test for 'deciding whether an expression is an illocution as distinct from a perlocution or neither'.

force intended by the speaker remains ambiguous after a consideration of the uttered sentence itself, even though what the
speaker means (on one interpretation) or a certain part of what
he means (on the other interpretation) is not at all ambiguous.
And even in those cases (e.g. 'I warn you that . . .') where the
intended force is not ambiguous, there is still a distinction to be
made (call it what you will) between (what Austin calls) meaning and (what Austin calls) force, though in these cases the distinction is a distinction at the level of abstraction only.

(3) In order for an illocutionary act to succeed, it is necessary
for the speaker to 'secure uptake', which Austin characterizes
as 'bringing about the understanding of the meaning and of the
force of the locution' (p. 116). An utterance of 'It's about to
charge' will not be the performance of an illocutionary act of
warning someone that the bull is about to charge unless the
audience to which the utterance is addressed takes it to be a
warning.[11] It is not necessary that the audience actually *heed* the
warning, for he might remain unconvinced that the bull actually is about to charge. But he must at least recognize that the
speaker intended his utterance to count as a warning: he must
recognize that the utterance was *issued as* a warning.

(4) Austin said that illocutionary acts are essentially *conventional* acts, where the conventions involved are not, apparently,
simply the linguistic conventions relevant to the constitution of
the locutionary act. Quite clearly, a large number of illocutionary
acts (e.g. promising, bequeathing, betting) include among their
constitutive conditions conventions of this sort: conventions
which define the practice of promising, betting, and the like.
But, as Strawson has pointed out, there are also many illocutionary acts which do not involve conventions in this sense at all:
acts such as asserting, objecting, etc.[12] So the exploitation of
conventions over and above the conventions of the language
itself does not seem to be a general constitutive condition for

[11] Of course, the speaker may be his own audience. If, seeing a buttercup while
alone on a walk, I say 'There's a buttercup', I have presumably made an assertion.
But I have 'secured uptake' only vacuously, in myself. 'Utterances addressed to
oneself' pose special problems of explanation which are not crucially relevant here.
Generally speaking, however, it seems both correct and to the point to say that the
possibility of addressing illocutionary acts to oneself depends upon the existence
of the 'institution' of inter-personal communication. And it is in terms of the latter
that the core of the explanation of illocutionary acts is to be provided.

[12] 'Intention and Convention in Speech Acts', loc. cit.

the performance of illocutionary acts, but a condition of this sort will be among the necessary conditions of a large and important class of illocutionary acts.

To perform an illocutionary act, then, a speaker must at least (1) perform a locutionary act L (2) intend L to have in the circumstances force F (3) secure uptake, and (4) in some cases, satisfy certain additional 'practice-defining' conventions.

Another way Austin provides for distinguishing locutionary from illocutionary acts is via a consideration of cases in which one of the acts is 'happy' while the other is not. Here are four kinds of infelicity which might occur at the locutionary–illocutionary border.

Force ambiguity. In this sort of case, a particular locution is capable of being used in the performance of more than one type of illocutionary act. In order to render the force unambiguous, a further specification is needed of the speaker's intention with respect to condition (2) above. Professor Searle's example, 'I'm going to do it', is a case in point. What the speaker means *by* his utterance may be clear enough. What is not clear is whether he means it as a threat or a promise or a prediction, etc.[13] The intended force might not be ambiguous if the utterance is considered in its conversational context, but this is not always the case.

Force misfire. The speaker intends to perform a particular illocutionary act, but for some reason it is void, despite the fact that he has said something meaningful in the determinate sense. Examples would be speaking too softly or in words the audience doesn't understand (failure to secure uptake), addressing one's remarks to the wrong person, or saying what one says at the wrong time or in the wrong place or in an inappropriate social context (failure to satisfy condition (4) above).

Phatic locutionary ambiguity. In this type of case, the force is unambiguous and uptake has been secured, and we may suppose that any relevant conventions have been duly exploited. Thus the illocutionary act succeeds. Yet the speaker may have mispronounced the words or mis-executed the utterance of the sentence in some other way, with the result that it is unclear to his audience just *what* he said. For example, suppose someone

---

[13] The ambiguity may, of course, be intended. As Searle points out, force may be more or less determinate, and so ambiguity of force is not *necessarily* unhappy.

says to me, in the presence of someone I recognize (from his picture) to be Professor Spratt, 'I should like you to meet Professor . . .' (at this point the speaker is seized with a coughing fit). But I know that it is Spratt standing before me, and I knew in advance that I was to be introduced. So the introduction succeeds. Or again, a drill sergeant shouts unintelligibly to some recruits on the parade field. It may be clear to them all that he has issued an order, but entirely unclear what he has ordered them to do.

Rhetic locutionary ambiguity. The drill sergeant has given an order. He said, quite distinctly, 'Pick it up, soldier!' But whom did he order? There were several soldiers present. And what did he order to be done? Did he, for instance, order someone to retrieve that cigarette-end, or to lift that packing case, or did he (in American military dialect) order some soldier to move more quickly? Unless the speaker's *SR*-intention is recognized, what he means by his utterance will not be recognized, even though the intended illocutionary force is recognized.

Although breakdowns may rarely occur in everyday speech situations, it is important to investigate them. For breakdowns help to illuminate the distinction between the locutionary act of saying what one says and the illocutionary act performed in saying what one says, which might go unnoticed in the normal successful speech act, where this distinction can usually be made only at the level of abstraction, as a 'distinction of reason'. But even in these cases the acts *are* different, according to Austin's account. For they have different constitutive conditions. It is only when meaning and force 'come apart' that the normally (merely) abstract acts have a life of their own.

II

Professor Searle's initial objection to Austin's doctrine is that the distinction Austin draws between locutionary and illocutionary acts 'cannot be completely general, in the sense of marking off two mutually exclusive classes of acts' (p. 143). The distinction works well enough in cases where the sentence uttered is ambiguous with respect to force (e.g. 'I'm going to do it'), since meaning and force appear to 'come apart' in these cases. But there are many sentences, including all those involving the performative use of illocutionary verbs, (e.g. 'I promise that I'm going to do it'), the *meaning* of which *determines* force in any literal, serious, and successful utterance. In such cases, 'the description of the act as a happily performed locutionary act—since it involves the meaning of the sentence—is already a description of the illocutionary act' (p. 143). Professor Searle concedes that 'the *concept* of an utterance with a certain meaning (i.e. the concept of a locutionary act) is indeed different from the *concept* of an utterance with a certain force (i.e. the concept of an illocutionary act' (p. 144). But the conceptual difference will not preserve the generality of the distinction, because there are cases in which the *class* of illocutionary acts contains members of the *class* of locutionary acts. In cases such as these, 'the attempt to abstract the locutionary meaning from illocutionary force would be like abstracting unmarried men from bachelors' (p. 144).

Why does Professor Searle consider this to be a difficulty? Austin was, after all, aware that not all utterances are ambiguous with respect to force. He did remark more than once that both classes of act are (except in certain 'breakdown' situations) merely abstractions from the total speech act. The fact (if it is a fact) that meaning sometimes determines force would not itself seem to constitute an objection to Austin's taxonomy. In any case, is the claim that the two concepts denote overlapping classes correct? The distinction between locutionary and illocutionary acts, as Austin understood it, is the distinction between the act of saying something and the act (e.g. promising or predicting) a speaker performs in saying what he says. An effective way of drawing attention to this distinction is to present examples in which the divergence between meaning and force shows a contrast between the locutionary and the illocutionary act. And this contrast is most obvious in those cases in which the sentence uttered is ambiguous with respect to force. However, even when meaning and force do not so obviously 'come apart', the distinction between the two speech acts can still be made. For even if there are cases in which meaning completely determines force, it isn't the *same thing* as force. One can always abstract the act of meaningfully saying 'I promise to do it' as an ancillary act involved in the performance of the total speech act without having to draw attention to the fact that saying

these words *in the appropriate circumstances* counts as the performance of the act of promising to do whatever it is. Therefore,
although it is true that in many cases the distinction is a distinction at the level of abstraction only—and Austin does say that
'to perform a locutionary act is in general . . . also and *eo ipso*
to perform an illocutionary act' (p. 198)—the generality of the
distinction is not affected. The distinction would lack generality
only if it were construed as being nothing other than, and
nothing more than, the distinction between the meaning of an
utterance and its force. Professor Searle's discussion of the distinction suggests that he tends to construe the distinction in this
way. But this is surely a misrepresentation of Austin's views.

Different kinds of ancillary act within the total speech act are
distinguished by different sets of constitutive conditions or
rules. To show that the distinction between locutionary and
illocutionary acts is completely general it is sufficient to point
out that the constitutive conditions for the performance of an
illocutionary act, though they include the constitutive conditions of the corresponding locutionary act, include other conditions as well.[14] Professor Searle has a low opinion of this line
of argument, objecting that this way of making the distinction
reduces it to a distinction between 'that part of trying to perform an illocutionary act which consists in uttering the sentence
seriously with its literal meaning, and actually succeeding in
performing an illocutionary act' (p. 145), a distinction which is,
though quite general, much less interesting than the 'original'
distinction between an utterance with a certain meaning and
an utterance with a certain force.

But the force of this objection is merely rhetorical. For the
constitutive conditions for the performance of any act may be
called the 'success conditions' for that act. To state what constitutes a checkmate in chess is to state the conditions such that,
if one satisfied them, one would succeed in checkmating one's opponent. Similarly, the constitutive conditions for a locutionary
act are the conditions for the successful performance of that
speech act. To talk about an utterance thus far and in these

---

[14] This is similar to the way in which the conditions for the performance of a
phatic act, for example, include the conditions for the performance of the corresponding phonetic act: every phatic act is a phonetic act, but not every phonetic
act is a phatic act.

respects is to talk about an utterance with a certain meaning. If the utterance fulfils certain other conditions as well, it constitutes the performance of a certain illocutionary act. And to talk about the utterance thus far and in these respects is to talk about an utterance with a certain force. But these additional, illocutionary conditions include the condition that the speaker must secure uptake: what he intends as a request, for instance, must be understood as such by his audience. But if an utterance's actually having the force of a request is contingent upon the success of the illocutionary act,[15] then the meaning of a seriously uttered sentence can never be said to determine the force of the utterance completely. It can at most completely determine its force-potential. Therefore, the distinction between (a certain part of) trying to perform an illocutionary act and actually succeeding is identical with the distinction between an utterance with a certain meaning and an utterance with a certain force. And if they are identical, the former cannot be less interesting, nor more general, than the latter. The distinction between meaning and force—between the meaning *of* an utterance and the force *of* an utterance—may indeed be less general than the distinction between locutionary and illocutionary acts. But that is a different distinction, which Austin used in order to draw attention to the distinction between the two kinds of act.

Having established to his satisfaction that there is no general distinction between locutionary and illocutionary acts, Professor Searle proceeds to argue that there is no distinction at all of the sort Austin had in mind. The focus of his attack here is the notion of a rhetic act. When contrasting locutionary and illocutionary acts, Austin uses the *oratio recta* form for reporting locutionary acts and the *oratio obliqua* form for reporting illocutionary acts. However, when he delimits the internal structure of locutionary acts, he uses *oratio recta* in his reports of phatic acts and *oratio obliqua* for reporting rhetic acts. The difficulty arises from the

---

[15] Austin is not clear on this point. Sometimes he talks as if an utterance has force *F* if and only if an illocutionary act of type *F* is successfully performed. At other times, he talks as if an utterance may have force *F* even if the illocutionary act does not succeed. Searle accepts the former interpretation, (see footnote 5 of his paper). But on the latter interpretation, of course, there is still a general distinction between illocutionary acts (with force *F*) and illocutionary acts of type *F*. It is only the claim that the distinction between meaning and force is completely general that must be abandoned if this latter interpretation is accepted.

fact that the verb-phrases Austin uses in indirect reports of rhetic acts always contain illocutionary verbs. This shows that rhetic acts cannot be characterized or reported except as illocutionary acts. It is true that they are very general illocutionary acts, (e.g. told to, asked whether, said that), but they are illocutionary none the less. Thus, 'There is no way to give an indirect report of a rhetic act . . . which does not turn the report into a report of an illocutionary act' (p. 147). No sentence, therefore, is completely force-neutral. Even such sentences as 'I'm going to do it' have some illocutionary force-potential built into their meaning. Consequently, 'on the characterization Austin has so far given us of locutionary as opposed to illocutionary acts, there are . . . no rhetic acts as opposed to illocutionary acts at all' (p. 148). But if there are no rhetic acts, the distinction between locutionary and illocutionary acts collapses; for 'it now emerges that *all* the members of the class of locutionary acts . . . are members of the class of illocutionary acts' (pp. 148–9). In the case of allegedly force-neutral utterances, meaning determines force only within broad limits, but it determines it nevertheless. In cases such as these, the force intended by the speaker may go beyond the literal meaning of the sentence. But this distinction between what the sentence means and what the speaker means in its utterance

has no special relevance to the general theory of illocutionary forces, because intended illocutionary force is only one of the aspects (sense and reference are others) in which intended speaker meaning may go beyond literal sentence meaning (p. 149).

The necessity of using illocutionary verbs in indirect reports of rhetic acts does, certainly, seem to suggest that the report of any rhetic act is the report of a (very general) illocutionary act. But it is rash to conclude from this feature of these reports that there are no rhetic acts, or that the distinction between locutionary and illocutionary acts is unsound. For this potentially embarrassing feature can be seen for the red herring it is once the rationale for, and the limitations of, the *oratio recta* and *oratio obliqua* formulae for reporting utterances are clearly recognized.

A standard rationale for employing the *oratio recta* form of report, in contrast with a report in *oratio obliqua*, is to allow the reporter to indicate that he is not, in his report, committing himself to be, so to speak, telling the whole story about what the original speaker said. The way he avoids this commitment is to repeat the words actually uttered by the original speaker, without giving any indication of any further import the utterance of those words may have had, or the original speaker may have intended his utterance to have. Austin used *oratio recta* to report phatic acts because he wished to focus on that aspect of the speaker's utterance in which meaning is determinable, not determinate. We often in fact use this form of report in everyday conversation when we are uncertain about the sense and/or reference of what the speaker said. We restrict our commitment by reporting only his pheme. By contrast, an *oratio obliqua* report commits the reporter to the claim of having understood more with respect to the reported utterance, by providing indications of sense and reference.[16] On the other hand, we may be prepared to indicate in our report what the speaker said inclusive of sense and reference, but we may be unwilling to commit ourselves to any definite indication of the force—actual or intended—of the original speaker's utterance. In such cases, we might naturally use *oratio recta* as a means of reporting the speaker's simple meaningful utterance and reserve *oratio obliqua* for those cases in which we are prepared to commit ourselves to an indication of the force of his utterance. Whether we are, in using these linguistic devices, contrasting phatic with rhetic acts or locutionary with illocutionary acts will usually be evident, in the conversational context, by our choice of *verbs* in our *oratio recta* reports. The difference in the two uses of these formulae is, therefore, entirely a difference in focus: a difference which will normally be evident within the context in which the report is made. Hence the recognition that an utterance may be meaningful, and worth reporting, even if the intended force is ambiguous (or even if the intended illocutionary act has completely misfired) provides the rationale for the use of *oratio recta* for reporting locutionary acts, just as the recognition that sense and/or reference may be ambiguous or otherwise defective provides a rationale for the use of *oratio recta* for reports of phatic acts.

---

[16] It will not go unnoticed that a report in this form also invariably, and unavoidably, provides at least some indication as to force, because the verbs used in such reports are always 'illocutionary verbs'. This is the red herring. I shall endeavour to dispose of it in the next paragraph. For the moment, let it swim.

These reportorial devices, however, have their limitations. For we must make do with only two formulae for reporting four types of speech act. *Oratio recta* is used to report both phatic and locutionary acts, *oratio obliqua* to report both rhetic and illocutionary acts. It is this dual role that has misled Professor Searle into thinking that rhetic acts and locutionary acts do not exist. But, as we have seen, rhetic acts are *purely abstract* in a way that the other acts in Austin's taxonomy are not. They have no 'independent existence' (which is not to say that they have no existence at all). Naturally enough, then, our language contains no 'rhetic verbs', and consequently other verbs have to be co-opted for use in *oratio obliqua* reports of rhetic acts.[17] The use of these verbs in indirect reports thus tends to suggest that illocutionary acts are being reported, if the reports are considered apart from their conversational contexts, for both the verbs and the *oratio obliqua* formula are also used to report full-blooded illocutionary acts. But the difficulty here is a difficulty only at the level of *reporting* rhetic acts. A rhetic act is *constituted* by the speaker's utterance of a pheme with (more or less definite) *SR*-intentions. The limitation language places upon the reports of these acts does not, therefore, indicate any fishiness in the *bona fides* of the acts themselves.

To sum up: (1) a rhetic act is that act constituted by a phatic act, plus *SR*-intentions; (2) because of the disambiguating role of this ancillary act, it is reported in *oratio obliqua* in contrast with the *oratio recta* report of the corresponding phatic act; (3) no additional conditions have to be met in order for a rhetic act to constitute a locutionary act, since every rhetic act includes a phatic act, which includes a phonetic act; (4) thus, a rhetic act, when considered as including these lower-level acts (as opposed to considering it in contrast with them), just is a locutionary act, from another classificatory point of view; (5) but every locutionary act, if otherwise felicitous, is also and *eo ipso* an illocutionary act; (6) hence it is proper to report rhetic acts in *oratio obliqua*, even though locutionary acts, because of the contrast with illocutionary acts, are properly reported in *oratio recta*. The

[17] The reportorial difficulty could be avoided altogether, by adopting an alternative form of report Austin used for locutionary acts, though this would perhaps make the contrasts he had in mind less perspicuous. A phatic act could be reported thus: 'He said: "Shoot her"', and the corresponding rhetic act thus: 'He said: "Shoot her", meaning by "shoot" shoot, and referring both by "her", to her.'

necessity of using 'illocutionary verbs' in indirect reports of rhetic acts thus points to the close conceptual ties between these different ancillary speech acts without in the least damaging the distinction between locutionary and illocutionary acts. This necessity would constitute an embarrassment for Austin's analysis only if he were committed, as we have seen that he is not, to the view that rhetic acts are ever *more* than mere abstractions. Therefore, Professor Searle's claim that the distinction between locutionary and illocutionary acts collapses because reports of rhetic acts must contain illocutionary verbs is mistaken, unless he wishes to argue for the principle that anything abstractly distinguishable must be capable of existing distinct 'in nature'.

The fact that indirect reports of rhetic acts always contain illocutionary verbs does show, as Professor Searle claims, that 'every sentence has some illocutionary force-potential, if only of a very broad kind, built into its meaning' (p. 148). And we have seen that the basic principles underlying Austin's classification of speech acts reflect this fact. However, an account is needed of the specific—or determinate—force of an utterance, in addition to the broad determination of force-potential which can be accounted for in terms of the meanings of sentences. For although no sentence is completely force-neutral, many utterances are nevertheless force-ambiguous. On my interpretation of Austin's doctrine this can be accounted for in terms of the relevant intentions of the speaker, which are among the constitutive features of those ancillary speech acts in which force-potential is determined. In those cases in which a verb has only one 'literal meaning' (e.g. 'promise'), the pheme determines the force-potential of the utterance and restricts the speaker's *SR*-intention (to mean *by* 'I promise to . . .' that he promises to . . .), and thus a serious and literal utterance of this sentence must be meant as a promise. In those cases, however, in which the 'literal meaning' of the sentence does not fully restrict the force-potential of the utterance (e.g. 'I'm going to do it', or 'It's going to charge'), the speaker's intention (to promise to do it, to warn him it's going to charge) serves this purpose.

Professor Searle, however, thinks that the distinction between the literal meaning of a sentence and the intended force of its utterance is 'only a special case' of the distinction between literal meaning and intended meaning, which 'has no special relevance to the general theory of illocutionary forces, because intended illocutionary force is only one of the aspects (sense and reference are others) in which intended speaker-meaning may go beyond literal sentence-meaning' (p. 149). But here Professor Searle seems to have confused determinable meaning (the meaning of a pheme) and determinate meaning (the meaning of a rheme). It is true that intended sense and reference can go beyond 'literal' sense and reference, where 'literal' is understood as 'determinable'. But intended sense and reference is what determines 'literal' sentence-meaning, if 'literal' is understood as 'determinate'. The same considerations apply to force. Since it is a necessary condition for an uttered sentence's having a certain force that the speaker intends it to have that force, the speaker's intentions in this respect are far from irrelevant to 'the general theory of illocutionary forces'. Of course, according to Professor Searle's 'Principle of Expressibility', it is possible in principle to avoid ambiguous sentences altogether. 'Whenever one wishes to make an utterance with force F, it is always possible to utter a sentence the meaning of which expresses exactly force F' (p. 153). That is, it is possible in principle always to utter a sentence the meaning of which makes it an adequate vehicle for expressing one's intentions quite unambiguously. But if the task of a theory of speech acts is to account for actual human communication rather than some idealized version of it, then we seem to require a taxonomical device to account for the (perhaps regrettable) fact that we do manage to perform illocutionary acts in the utterance of sentences that are not, in terms of their 'literal meaning', unambiguous in this respect. That 'said-meaning' and 'meant-force' do come apart is, as Searle claims, merely a contingent fact about the way that we speak; but that they *can* come apart is a conceptual truth accounted for by the distinction Austin draws between locutionary and illocutionary acts.

III

Although Professor Searle thinks that Austin's distinction between locutionary and illocutionary acts is not tenable, he does think that certain 'real' distinctions underlie Austin's efforts. One of these—the distinction between the propositional content of an utterance and its force or illocutionary type—is singled out for special attention as a distinction that is partially to supplant Austin's distinction.

Utterances with divergent illocutionary forces (e.g. 'John, leave the room!', 'Will John leave the room?' and 'John will leave the room') often have a common 'content', which some philosophers have called the *proposition* expressed in the utterance. Since the proposition can not be identified with the whole sentence uttered, but only with those constituents of it which contain no indicators of illocutionary force, the proposition (and the corresponding propositional act: the act of expressing the proposition) are said to be 'genuine abstractions from the illocutionary act'. Since the proposition is that part of any uttered sentence which involves 'correspondence with the facts', the distinction between propositional and illocutionary acts can help explain Austin's remark that when we are concerned with 'constatives' we abstract as much as possible from the illocutionary aspects of an utterance and concentrate on the locutionary aspects, whereas when we are concerned with 'performatives' we abstract from the locutionary aspects and concentrate on the illocutionary force of the utterance.

A problem facing anyone who wishes to make use of the admittedly attractive notion of a proposition is to find a way of characterizing the nature of propositions precisely and of describing just how they function in speech acts. Professor Searle does not discuss these questions in much detail in the paper under consideration, but a more detailed discussion of propositions is to be found in 'What is a Speech Act?'[18] Expressing a proposition, he tells us there, involves the subsidiary acts of *referring* to someone or something and of *predicating* some property or act or what-not of that to which one has referred. Thus, in uttering the two sentences: 'John will leave the room', and 'John, leave the room', the speaker refers to John and predicates leaving the room of him. He expresses the same proposition in both utterances. The difference between the utterances is accounted for by the different force-indicators in each sentence, which indicators may be semantical or syn-

---

[18] Op. cit., pp. 225–7.

tactical or phonological. Returning to his later paper: 'Symbolically, we might represent the sentence as containing an illocutionary force-indicating device and a propositional content indicator. Thus: $F(p)$, where the range of possible values for F will determine the range of illocutionary force, and the p is a variable over the infinite range of possible propositions' (p. 156).

Although the notion of a proposition can be a very helpful analytic tool, its proper function is not, I think, to help supplant the distinction between locutionary and illocutionary acts but rather to help supplement it. The significance of the notion derives from the assumption that human communication is not miraculous: the assumption, that is, that everything an audience needs to know in order to understand the meaning of a speaker's utterance and to discover its intended illocutionary force must either be presented 'in' the utterance itself or be available for inspection in the context. The analysis of the speaker's utterance (his locution) in terms of propositional content-indicators and force-indicators enables us to explain how this requirement is met. It enables us to provide a linguistic analysis of the features of the speaker's uttered sentence which enable his audience to identify the content of the message and to discover the speaker's intentions as to illocutionary force. The speaker may choose to make his intentions with respect to sense, reference, and force quite explicit by including sufficient indicators in the sentence he utters to render it completely unambiguous in these respects (e.g. by the use of an explicit performative preface, by using proper names instead of pronouns, etc.), or by accompanying his utterance with suitable gestures, etc. But the speaker's uttered sentence does not always contain explicit indicators of propositional content and force, and in such cases the audience has to rely on features of the context of the utterance (e.g. the relative social position of speaker and audience, the topic of the conversation, etc.) in order to 'figure out' the speaker's intentions in these respects.

Since the uttered sentence contains propositional content-indicators and (at least some) force-indicators, this important feature of communication needs to be accounted for in the taxonomy of speech acts. Hence the act of expressing a proposition: the propositional act. But notice that this ancillary speech act does not *replace* the locutionary act; for expressing a proposition is not the same thing as uttering a meaningful sentence (in the determinate sense), and I have argued that the illocutionary act cannot be identified with the act of uttering a meaningful sentence. Where, then, do propositional acts reside? Austin provides a helpful clue. It will be remembered that Austin subdivides the rhetic act into the subsidiary acts of naming and referring (p. 97). The referring involved here is determined by the speaker's intention which disambiguates the referring expression contained in the pheme. Professor Searle's act of referring seems to perform the same function ('the speaker *refers* to a particular person John . . .'). Furthermore, in any sentence with determinate meaning, the predicate must also be determinate ('the speaker . . . *predicates* the act of leaving the room of that person'). Consequently, there seems to be ample justification for including an additional subsidiary act—the act of predication—within the rhetic act, which would make the propositional act (the act of referring and predicating) also a subsidiary act within the rhetic act. Thus, in performing a rhetic act, we may now say, the speaker (*a*) utters a meaningful sentence (in the determinate sense); and in so doing he (*b*) expresses a proposition. He also, of course, (*c*) provides at least some indication, in the sentence he utters, of the intended force of his utterance. This re-interpretation of the rhetic act elucidates the sense in which the (determinate) meaning of an uttered sentence determines at least some (and sometimes all) of the illocutionary force-potential of the utterance. It also shows how Professor Searle's valuable notion of a propositional act can be accommodated within Austin's basic classificatory scheme. Furthermore, it is fully in line with Austin's remark that a locutionary act is also, 'in general and *eo ipso*', an illocutionary act.

IV

Armed with the distinction between propositional acts and illocutionary acts, Professor Searle mounts an attack, in the final section of his paper, on Austin's often criticized views concerning truth. The point of his attack is that Austin was guilty of a confusion concerning the nature of statements, and that this confusion was responsible for his mistaken view that illocutionary acts are the bearers of truth or falsity.

As many philosophers have noticed, 'statement' is structurally ambiguous, meaning either the act of stating or the product of the act of stating. It shares this form of ambiguity with many (perhaps most) other nominalized forms of illocutionary verbs. For instance, when one performs the illocutionary act of promising, what one produces is a promise. But the expression 'your promise' can be used to refer either to your act of promising or to its content or product: what you promised. Similarly, 'Remember my warning', can mean either *remember my warning you* or *remember what I warned you about*. Indeed, 'speech act' and 'illocutionary act' are themselves ambiguous in this way, as is 'act': all share the 'act–object' ambiguity.

Was Austin guilty of confusion on this point? It must be admitted that Austin did not *state*, in so many words, that 'statement' is structurally ambiguous in this way. But there is ample evidence, in 'Truth'[19] and in *How to Do Things with Words*, that he was aware of the distinction and relied on it in his discussion of truth. Consider, for a start, his remarks on page 138 of *How to Do Things with Words*:

> Once we realize that what we have to study is *not* the sentence but the issuing of an utterance in a speech situation, there can hardly be any longer a possibility of not seeing that stating is performing an act.

Perhaps it is this remark, or remarks like it, that lead Professor Searle to conclude that Austin missed the distinction, and thought that the act of stating is what is true or false. But on the next page, after a brief consideration of some conditions an utterance has to meet in order to count as an illocutionary act of stating something, Austin says:

> Let us agree that all these circumstances of situation have to be in order for me to have succeeded in stating something, yet when I have, *the* question arises, was what I stated true or false? And this we feel . . . is now the question of whether the statement 'corresponds with the facts' (p. 139).

[19] Consider, for instance: 'A statement is made, and its making is an historic event (p. 87); 'A statement may refer to "itself" in the sense . . . of the sentence used or the utterance uttered in making it ("statement" is not exempt from all ambiguity' (p. 94, footnote 2). See also page 90, paragraph 1 and footnote 3.

Here it seems perfectly clear that the expression 'the statement'
is meant to refer to 'what I stated', or what Searle calls the
statement-object. And this is *contrasted* with stating, which is said
to be the performance of an act. Again, with respect to *utterances*
('utterance' has the same structural ambiguity as 'statement'):

There is no necessary conflict between (*a*) our issuing the utterance
being the doing of something, (*b*) our utterance being true or false
(p. 134).

Austin continually contrasts the making of a statement with the
statement thus made, the issuing of an utterance with what is
thus uttered. And it is the latter in each case that is always said
to be true or false.[20] Austin, then, was in full agreement with the
view that statement-objects—not statement-acts or 'speech
episodes'—are what are true or false.

But if this was Austin's view, why all his fuss about stating
being the performance of an act? Why do statement-acts loom
so large in his discussion of truth? One reason, I think, is this.
In order to *assess* a statement for truth or falsity, we have to
determine its identity: we have to determine, that is, *just what*
has been stated. And to determine this is to identify the determinate sense and reference of the statement. (To be able to
determine whether 'The cat is on the mat' is true, we have
to determine which cat is being said to be on which mat.) And to
determine *this* is to determine the speaker's *intentions* with respect
to sense and reference, as expressed in his statement-act.[21] So,
to assess a statement as true or false, we have to consider it as
the product of a (perhaps imagined or possible) statement-act.
Now Searle seems to realize this: for he says that the statement-
object is what is stated, *construed as stated*, which is identical with
the *proposition*, *construed as stated* (as opposed to being construed
as asked, construed as commanded, etc.). But to construe a
proposition as stated is to construe it as (a constituent of) the

[20] True, Austin does sometimes talk about *stating truly*. But here there is no reason
to take the act as the bearer of truth. To say that someone stated truly that *p* is
just to say that he stated that *p* and that what he stated is true.

[21] When we assess what some particular person has actually stated, we have to
determine what his *SR*-intention actually was. But sometimes we are concerned
with the truth or falsity of statements not actually made by anyone, but which
could or might be (or have been) made by someone. And in these cases too we
have to consider the statement determinate in sense and reference. But in these
cases it is *our* intentions which determine the identity of the statement.

product of a statement-act: namely, an illocutionary act of stating. However, as I pointed out earlier, 'illocutionary act' is subject to the same structural ambiguity as 'statement'. Thus we can say that illocutionary acts (= illocutionary act-objects) are what can be true or false, while denying that illocutionary acts (= illocutionary actings) can be true or false.

V

In this paper, I have argued that Professor Searle has not unearthed defects in Austin's analysis of speech acts which would necessitate the jettisoning of his basic distinction between locutionary and illocutionary acts. In so far as Professor Searle's objections touch on wider philosophical issues, 'such as the nature of statements, the way truth and falsity relate to statements, and the way what sentences mean relates to what speakers mean when they utter sentences', I hope I have given reason to believe that the Austinian framework is capable of treating these issues adequately.

Throughout my paper, I have relied heavily on an interpretation of Austin's doctrine which gives a large and important role to the intentions of speakers in distinguishing the various ancillary speech acts. Although I have taken pains to show that this interpretation is justified by what Austin actually says (though sometimes only implicitly), it seems to me to have independent justification, in the sense that it accounts for features of human communication which otherwise remain mysterious. Although I have distinguished several distinct intentions, these may be looked upon as abstractions, much in the same way that the ancillary speech acts are abstractions. It might, for some purposes, be better to say that, in the total speech act, one complex intention is operative. Whether we speak of one intention or many seems to me mere taxonomical preference.

Works Cited

G. E. M. ANSCOMBE, *Intention* (Blackwell, 1957).

ARISTOTLE, *Nicomachean Ethics*.

BRUCE AUNE, 'Hypotheticals and Can, another look', *Analysis* (1968).

—— 'Reply to Lehrer', *Analysis* (1970).

J. L. AUSTIN, *Philosophical Papers* (1st edn., Oxford, 1961; 2nd edn., Oxford, 1970).

—— *How to Do Things with Words* (Oxford, 1962).

—— *Sense and Sensibilia* (Oxford, 1962).

A. J. AYER, *Language, Truth and Logic* (Gollancz, 1936).

M. R. AYERS, *The Refutation of Determinism* (Methuen, 1968).

B. BEROFSKY (ed.), *Free Will and Determinism* (Harper & Row, 1966).

R. M. CHISHOLM, 'J. L. Austin's Philosophical Papers', *Mind* (1964).

N. CHOMSKY, *Syntactic Structures* (Mouton, 1957).

L. J. COHEN, 'Do Illocutionary Forces Exist?', *Philosophical Quarterly*, 14 (1964).

K. T. FANN (ed.), *Symposium on J. L. Austin* (Routledge, 1969).

G. FREGE, 'The Thought: A Logical Inquiry', trans. A. M. Quinton, *Mind* (1956).

—— *Foundations of Arithmetic*, trans. J. L. Austin (Blackwell, 1950).

H. P. GRICE, 'The Causal Theory of Perception', *Proceedings of the Aristotelian Society*, supp. vol. (1961).

—— 'Meaning', *Philosophical Review* (July 1957).

—— 'Utterer's Meaning, Sentence-Meaning and Word-Meaning', *Foundations of Language* (August 1968).

R. M. HARE, 'Some Alleged Differences between Imperatives and Indicatives', *Mind* (1967).

A. M. HONORÉ, 'Can and Can't', *Mind* (1964).

L. A. JACOBOVITS and D. D. STEINBERG (edd.), *Semantics* (Cambridge, 1971).

A. J. P. KENNY, *Action, Emotion and Will* (Routledge, 1961).

K. LEHRER (ed.), *Freedom and Determinism* (Random House, 1966).

—— 'Cans without Ifs', *Analysis* (1968).

C. I. LEWIS, *Mind and the World Order* (Scribner, 1929).

DON LOCKE, 'Ifs and Cans Revisited', *Philosophy* (1962).

N. MALCOLM, *Ludwig Wittgenstein: A Memoir* (Oxford, 1962).

M. MERLEAU-PONTY, *Phenomenology of Perception*, trans. C. Smith (Routledge, 1962).

G. E. MOORE, *Principia Ethica* (Cambridge, 1903).

—— *Ethics* (Pelican Books, 1952).

P. NOWELL-SMITH, 'Ifs and Cans', *Theoria* (1960); reprinted in Berofsky, op. cit.

B. RUSSELL, 'The Limits of Empiricism', *Proceedings of the Aristotelian Society* (1935–6).

G. RYLE, *The Concept of Mind* (Hutchinson, 1949).

—— 'Systematically Misleading Expressions', *Proceedings of the Aristotelian Society* (1931–2).

S. M. SCHIFFER, *Meaning* (Oxford, 1972).

J. R. SEARLE, 'What is a Speech Act?', in *Philosophy in America*, ed. M. Black (London, 1965).

—— *Speech Acts, An Essay in the Philosophy of Language* (Cambridge, 1969).

—— 'Assertions and Aberrations', in *British Analytical Philosophy*, edd. B. A. O. Williams and A. C. Montefiore (London, 1966).

P. F. STRAWSON, 'Phrase et acte de parole', *Langages*, 17 (mars 1970).

—— 'Intention and Convention in Speech Acts', *Philosophical Review* (October 1964); reprinted in *Logico-Linguistic Papers* (Methuen, 1971).

—— (and others), 'Truth', *Proceedings of the Aristotelian Society*, supp. vol. (1950).

I. THALBERG, 'Austin on Ability', in K. T. Fann, op. cit.

J. O. URMSON, 'J. L. Austin', in *Encyclopedia of Philosophy*, ed. P. Edwards (Random House, 1967).

G. J. WARNOCK, *English Philosophy since 1900* (2nd edn., Oxford University Press, 1969).

—— *The Object of Morality* (Methuen, 1971).

D. WIGGINS, 'On sentence-sense, word-sense and difference of word-sense', in Jacobovits and Steinberg, op. cit.

L. WITTGENSTEIN, *Tractatus Logico-Philosophicus* (Kegan Paul, 1922).

—— *The Blue and Brown Books* (Blackwell, 1958).

—— *Philosophical Investigations* (Blackwell, 1953).

Index